JUST
MARKET
IT

Sell More Books by Monetising Your Income Streams

Winsome Duncan

Published by

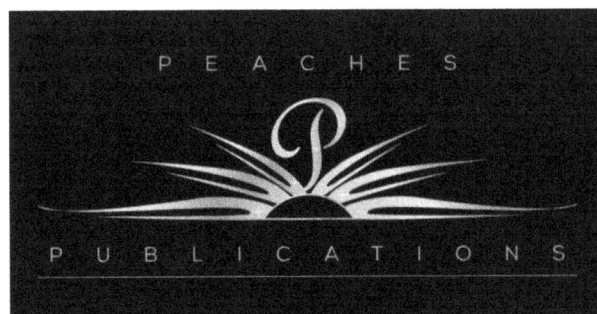

PEACHES

PUBLICATIONS

www.peachespublications.co.uk

Published in the United Kingdom by Peaches Publications, 2021.

www.peachespublications.co.uk

Stock images courtesy of: www.pixabay.com.

Text Copyright © 2021 by Winsome Duncan.

First Edition.

ISBN: 9781838147228.

British Library Cataloguing in Publication Data: A catalogue record for this book is available from the British Library.

Book cover design: Peaches Publications.

Typesetter: Winsome Duncan.

Editor: Winsome Duncan.

Proofreader: Linda Green.

Table of Contents

I Am An Author...i

Dedication...ii

Contract..iii

Acknowledgements...1

Foreword...3

Preface..6

Mr and Mrs Know-It-All...8

FOUNDATION STEPS..10

What is Your Why?...11

Gauging Your Commitment Levels 12

What Makes You an AUTHORity? 13

Press Life 15

The Rose Formula 22

Core Message 23

Foundation Steps to Passive Income 24

Concrete Footprints 25

Marketing Definition 26

Advertising and Promotional Definition 27

Amazon Author Central 28

The Author Brand Story 30

Six Book Formats..32

Six Ways to Monetise Your Book 35

Look Inside Feature 38

Pre-order 39

Get Organised and Mobilise 40

Creative Marketing Budget...41

Free ISBNs vs Paid ISBNs..43

Upgrade Your Mindset...44

Benefits of Word of Mouth...48

Social Media Accounts 49

Social Media Checklist...52

The Smoke and Mirror Illusion.......................................54

JUST MARKET IT 56

Starting A Book Business..57

Micro Business Plan 58

Identifying your Marketer Avatars 59

Identifying your Target Customer....................................62

Sample Target Buyer Profile 64

Your Target Buyer Reader Profile 65

Primary and Secondary Target Audience 66

Guerrilla Marketing...67

Relaunch..68

Mailing List 69

Lost Leaders 70

Do's and Don'ts of Marketing 71

99 Marketing Ideas for Growth 72

Testimonials 77

Selecting Your Marketing Campaign................................78

    4 Weeks Express Campaign 79

    8 Weeks Micro Campaign 84

    12 Weeks Standard Campaign 94

THE ROLLS ROYCE OF MARKETING 108

    Always Be Closing (ABC)... 109

    Low – Medium – High Price Points 110

    50 Call to Action Phases 112

    Copywriting 115

    Copywriting Sales Pitch 116

    A Compelling Call-to-Action Copy 117

    Call-To-Action Copy 118

    Prospects Require Attentive Listening................................ 119

    A Media Press Pack 121

    3D Book Placement Adverts 124

    Sample Press Release... 125

    Press Release Template 126

    Author Information (AI) 127

    Branding with Lily.. 129

HONEY IN YOUR MONEY.. 136

    Book Inventory... 137

    Card Readers.. 138

    Websites 139

    Landing Page 139

    Income Streams 140

    The World Is Your Stage... 142

    Public Presentation Skills 143

    Accountability Partner 143

    Book Embellishment 144

    Templates Are Your Best Friend 145

    Bulk Buy Book Sales 146

Sale on Return (SOR) 147

Outsourcing 147

Wholesalers List 148

Handling Rejection Like A Boss 150

Paid Advertising on Social Media 152

Increase Your Sales 30-day Challenge 155

Just Dominate 156

Committing to Win 158

How to Become an Amazon Number 1 Bestseller 161

Epilogue 164

References 165

About the Author 166

About Lily Naadu Mensah 169

The Popcorn House 170

Appendix *172*

Mind Mapping tools 173

Study Notes pages 180

I Am Author

This Just Market It workbook

belongs to author:

_____

Dedication

In loving memory of Barbara Campbell, thank you for giving me journalist wings to fly. My dearest friend, you will live on forever in my heart.

Rest in Sweet Peace, Babs.

XXX

XX

X

The Contract

I_____
(Insert your name above)

promise to level up and push my book business to the next level.

I understand that I need to learn new techniques and be dedicated to achieving all my marketing objectives.

This contract is an agreement with myself to complete and honour my marketing campaign in the year 20_____.

Signed: _____

Date: _____/_____/_____

Acknowledgements

First and foremost, I must thank God Almighty, who has walked me through what has sometimes been a journey of solitude within my writer's world. I give you the glory, I give you the honour! Fill me up so I can pour into others. Use me as your vessel until I am no more. Thank you for your abundant Grace that has taken me out of the depths of dark despair. I am all that I am simply because you are. Let there be more of you and less of me. Use me as your humble servant to emancipate our people and lead them to financial wealth with their book business. Let my black excellence always be a demonstration of the goodness and mercy you have ministered over my life. It is well, now, and forever more, Amen.

I would like to acknowledge and thank change for being ever-present in my life. Your consistency encourages me to get out of my comfort zone and demand more of myself every day. Thank you for allowing me to be a Change Agent. I believe a change is coming; things have got to change. Be the change you want to see in the world. As we turn the page into this new chapter in my life, I pray for continued abundant blessings upon blessings. It is well in my world.

I would like to thank my mum for always being there for me through thick and thin. A mother's love is like no other, and I am glad to have you in my corner, pushing me to be great. My love always.

I would like to thank my dear friend 'Boogles' also known as Lisa Newton of Boogles Accounting. You always listen to my nonsense. Thank you for allowing me to vent and getting me out of a tight space. I love and appreciate you as a lifelong friend; you cannot get rid of me, ever! I am here to stay.

A HUGE thank you goes out to the Peaches Publications team who help make this well-oiled machine work. I could not do this without the fabulous Editors, Proofreaders, Graphic Designers, Illustrators and vendors on board. You make me look good on social media platforms, but really there is no 'I' in teamwork.

A special acknowledgement to the phenomenal superwoman that is Joanna Oliver from Consult a Chameleon, your light is dazzling. Thank you for being my confidant in business and for our late-night giggles. I pray for God to enlarge your territory, you are so much more than a Bid Writer, Proofreader and Editor, you are my friend. A perfect note on a tight beat.

I would like to thank the two contributors to this book, Neusa Catoja and Lily Naadu Mensah, for handing in their pieces in record time. Neusa, aka 'The Book Slayer', it is an honour and a privilege to work with you on this project. To all our seven-figure dreams that we want to manifest, I breathe life into it, and I personally know it is only a matter of time before they are realised. To my darling style icon 'Lily Rose' (Lily Naadu Mensah), it has been a minute and oh boy, what a blessing it has been to know you. We can all agree that our health is our wealth and thank you for helping me tap into the riches unknown, which is sleep. For that, I will forever be indebted. Your passion about branding was prevalent at my award nomination at The House of Parliament. You paid detailed attention to clothing colours, jewellery and make up, you are super knowledgeable in the brand industry.

Okay, well, it is time to say goodbye and conclude this section of the book and be on my merry way. Only kidding. To all my beautiful clients, who have poured into my vision. I get to wake up daily and enjoy what I love— there are no more Blue Mondays. Every day, even if I am tired, I get up and I live the dream. Thank you for letting me be of service. Thank you for entrusting me with your amazing stories. I am honoured to know you all. I wish you the best in all your marketing endeavours.

Finally, a massive shout-out to EVERYONE who attended the online JUST WRITE IT SEMINARS and the TELL YOUR STORY, WRITE YOUR BOOK MASTER CLASSES. This is why we are here with me writing a book in just seven months because you challenged me to do so, and of course, I am going to rise to the occasion every time. I hope you enjoy and get a lot out of this. I wish you well in all that you do. Peace In.

Foreword

By Neusa Catoja

My name is Neusa Catoja, also known as The Book Slayer. I am a Transformation Coach and NLP practitioner. My company is called Free to Embrace Me.

I refer to Winsome Duncan as a Boss Queen! Her ability to create and open possibilities in authors' writing whilst they share their stories with the world is one of her superpowers. However, she has many undiscovered superpowers and hidden talents which she uses as a Book Confidence Coach.

Just Market It has been written to help newbie and established authors understand the complexities of marketing. She has a unique ability to use your story to inspire and encourage people to become loyal, returning customers. Whether you are selling your book, a product, a service or getting yourself out there as a brand, Boss Queen Winsome and her team can cover it all.

Her ideas are simple yet powerful. In one consultation, she can easily capture your vision for your service or product, and she shows you the potential avenues you can venture down. If you are an entrepreneur, she will enable you to see the possibility of a much bigger picture within your book business and increase your income streams. As a Thought Leader, Winsome supports her clients through the journey of being their best selves as authors.

Having the pleasure of my debut book, *Soul of a Woman – Journey to Self-Love,* published by her company, Peaches Publications, I got to see the magic she puts in the sauce up close and personal. I am also her accountability partner, and once a week, we have accountability calls to keep each other in check. We share ideas to promote our services, sell our books and create products which has enabled me to become a Number One, five-star bestseller on Amazon, create a coaching programme and even create merchandise; not only to place myself as an author but also as a trusted public brand.

Follow the direction in *Just Market It* fiercely. If you are currently struggling with sales, not reaching your target market, suffering from a lack of finances, or even unleashing the many ideas you have as a leader and entrepreneur, this will soon become your guide to solving ALL these problems. Trust me, by reading this workbook, you will soon understand the power of marketing and the beauty of upselling your products and services. Your job is to enjoy this process effortlessly and learn what you do not know. I highly recommend this book as I recommend her first book, *Just Write It,* for established authors who need a professional approach to their book business.

With Winsome's support, I have sold hundreds of copies of my books. My programmes and online workshops sell like hotcakes, and I absolutely love marketing and bringing out new products and services for my clients. Not to mention that I am now writing my second and third manuscripts. The book says what it means, *JUST MARKET IT* and tells it like it is. You will never see advertising and promotion as something to be feared; rather, as the solution to what your clients are seeking. Get excited, grab your pen, open your mind, and let her guide you to become a most wanted author and entrepreneur.

Let's slay it!

Neusa Catoja

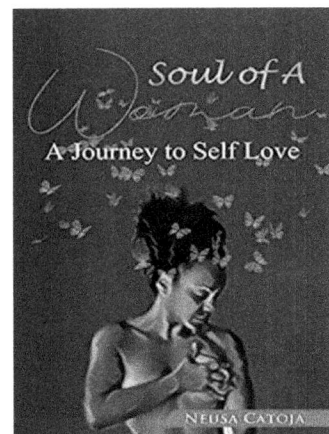

"The mind is like a parachute – it works best when open."

Frank Zappa

Preface

Are you one of those 'I tried everything' people?

In my experience over the past twenty years, I have learned the top seven key reasons why people do not market their books correctly. Take a look and see if any of these reasons sound familiar to you:

1. I have no budget
2. I am not very technical
3. I do not know what to say
4. My laptop or PC does not work
5. I cannot be bothered
6. It is too much work
7. I want to stay in my comfort zone

It is so sad to see money being left on the table along with dreams deferred. You must learn to require more of yourself and push your book business to new heights. In my experience when working with authors, the ones who invest in learning what they do not know have the following traits:

Just Market It

- ❖ A valid purpose
- ❖ Are in alignment with their calling
- ❖ Not afraid to step into unknown territory
- ❖ Risk takers
- ❖ Bold and brave
- ❖ Hardworking
- ❖ Obedient
- ❖ Teachable
- ❖ Attentive listening
- ❖ Take massive action
- ❖ Compliant
- ❖ A good student

How to use this workbook: To get the best from your workbook you need to study it all and complete all the exercises. Be proactive in each section and do not skip anything if you feel overwhelmed take a break and revisit it or outsource it to freelancer. Use the Mind Mapping tools, and Notes pages in the Appendix to help you. I have put a reference section together at the back of the book packed full of the useful services I use. Be sure to check each one out and learn about the benefits. Once you have graduated from this workbook and you feel confident to take the advance marketing module, I would like to invite you to attend my Sparkle N Shine Book Marketing online course. Join me on a six-week live training as I prepare you to take centre stage, have an appealing media presence, increase your likability factor, show you the benefits in building a book series, media positioning and client training packages. Sign up here: www.bookconfidencecoach.com.

Marketing your book is a serious matter; writing a book is the easy part. Selling it beyond your family and your friendship circle is the secret sauce. Expanding your core message globally is the next step. Always remember your word is your bond.

Happy marketing, prosperous, super selling and all that good stuff!

Mr and Mrs Know-It-All

When you make excuses about why you have not sold X number of books, etc, blah, blah, blah, the beauty in that is you get to keep ALL your excuses. My job as a Book Confidence Coach is to show you all the options, and let you make an informed choice. I am not here to coerce you; I do not fight, push, or pull with those who do not respect my knowledge or want to be shown the way. Arrogance will trip you up every step of the way when you think you know it all. I have worked with hundreds of clients in person and remotely, and arrogance is a shade that they do not wear well. If they know so much, why are they on the phone with me?

In my publishing agreements, I always state you must believe that I have the knowledge, skills, and expertise to take your book to the next level. When this kind of thing happens, I remain silent and just listen and note that this person is not my ideal client. We both cannot typeset the same book; if you are told the cover picture does not match the book content, please believe me. If you are so excellent at what you do and how good your book is, why do we even need to speak? I must draw a line here; I want to work with open-minded clients who appreciate my guidance and see the value in what I bring, not someone trying a thing and failing at it miserably! I mention this so you can have some self-reflection, and for a moment, just forget what you know and start from a blank page. Learn what you can and action your task to the best of your ability.

No one has done every diet. Neither have they tried everything when it comes to marketing their books, it is impossible. I often sit at the feet of authors and publishers who are more successful than I am and simply listen or invest in their training. I am listening for what I do not know and how I can do it better. I am wanting to be the best in the publishing industry and there is still so much more to teach you all. I have had authors with marketing degrees attend my workshop and masterclasses because they want to have a profound inside knowledge of the publishing industry. They have humbled themselves to want to learn more. How committed are you to the marketing process and learning something new? Be of good cheer, try and leverage what I am about to teach you in the best way possible. Yearn to become Mr and Mrs Want-To-Know-More.

"Everybody wants to be a beast until it is time to do what beasts do."

Eric Thomas

FOUNDATION STEPS

What is Your Why?

Let us quickly establish why you want to market your book effectively. I want to see whether you are only dipping your big toe into the marketing pool or if you are going to deep dive and fully immerse yourself into the ocean that is the world of marketing. I do not want you to drown out here, so see this workbook as your lifeline to staying afloat when it comes to selling your book.

As well as being all in 100%, your approach to marketing your book, product or service is: How can I upsell? Instead of selling one to one, how do I sell many to one? Although my niche market are authors in this book, most of these tips can be transferable. Really dig deep and think about what your motive was when purchasing a copy of this book. Please complete your five reasons why you want to market your book more effectively:

1 ....

....

2 ....

....

3 ....

....

4 ....

....

5 ....

....

Gauging Your Commitment Levels

Be honest with yourself. When you think about your schedule, commitments, the children, the family, friends, the husband, or the wife, what is your commitment level to marketing your book on a scale of 1 to 10?

1_____5_____10
 (Low)   (Medium)   (High)

1-3 – You probably will not read this book and will instead place it on the shelf somewhere in the house. It is okay, now is simply not the right time; I see you have a lot going on. Just try and reflect on these pages when you feel led. Worst-case scenario, pass it forward to another author who would benefit. Do not keep this gem to yourself.

4-7 – You are on the road to middling and are very curious about learning new innovative marketing skills; however, something always gets in the way. You start well but cannot finish. 'Easy does it' is not the space required for creating marketing campaigns. Try and get a little more focus and push yourself and your skillset to an 8, please.

8-10 – You are indeed ready to roll, so let go. You are in it for the long distance. And win, lose or draw, you will be here to see this thing through. You have the will, grit, and determination to finish what you started. You are fearless, and even if you are a newbie marketer, you want to learn so much more. You follow instructions and have the pizazz to get to bestseller status, so keeping pushing and try and get the perfect 10 score!

What Makes You an AUTHORity?

I want you to imagine what it would be like to get loads of press coverage for your book. Think about how big your smile would be. When you get up in the morning, you feel refreshed and ready to go to the next level. Dream a marketing dream that scares you. Look beyond the ideas of conforming that society has placed on you. Be that author that sells more than the average 300 copies of your book in its lifetime. Step out of your comfort zone and be bold with your book business.

Let us get really clear from the starting gate. I am undoubtedly a BOSS CHICK all day long! I was not born this way; I learned the skills on the hard road of being an entrepreneur. It has not been an easy road, but it is well worth it now that I have reached a time when I love the skin that I am in. I am the type of woman who, if I hear the word 'no', it just falls on deaf ears. I keep pushing until I can get a 'yes'. I am extremely focused and hardworking, but words are not enough. I am not trying to be braggadocious here with a big ego; I am self-full, and I am filling myself with all the knowledge I can to make my publishing job as easy as possible. My work speaks for itself; the following press life page is a small snippet of the press coverage I have had as an author. I am about my brand, and it is important to grab whatever opportunity arises, that is within your alignment, with both hands. I am also a multi-award winner of seven awards, and I pride myself on excellence in all I do, and you should too. I have included a small number of my press clippings which positions me to be the go-to person when it comes to marketing your books.

It is now time for you to uncover what your AUTHORity in your field is and to begin to unpack how you can move forward in your author journey. Remember to be bold and confident and think about all aspects of your skillset. This exercise is not for the meek or mild—get hands-on.

Just Market It

It is important to identify why the media should spotlight your work. Write down three key areas that make you an AUTHORity in your field of expertise and why.

Key AUTHORity Areas:

Key Area 1	
Why?	
Key Area 2	
Why?	
Key Area 3	
Why?	

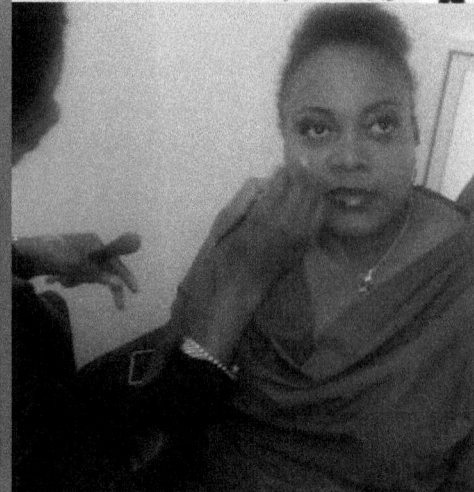

Press Life

Adding water inspired me to beat my credit crunch

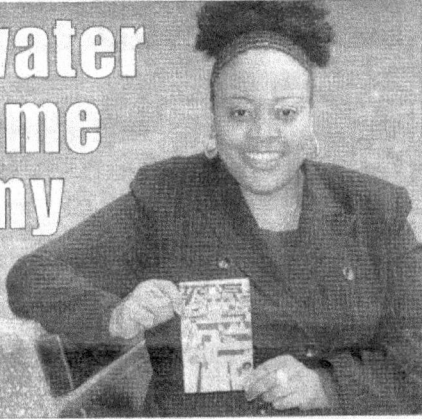

NOVEL IDEAS: Winsome Duncan with her book, also inset

AUTHOR TELLS HOW YOU CAN BEAT YOURS...

By OLIVER PORRITT

A PERFORMANCE poet who beat her own personal credit crunch has written a book full of tips to help people on the breadline.

Winsome Duncan, 33, from Bermondsey, has written her guide to cost-effective living featuring more than 100 ways of becoming more financially savvy.

An Inner City Guide To Surviving The Credit Crunch will be launched at Peckham Library on October 1.

Ms Duncan started writing down her ideas in October, 2010, but the origins of the book go back five-and-a-half years.

She said: "I was redundant and going through a low in my life but one small event changed my outlook.

"The liquid hand soap was basically empty. But I added some water to the dispenser and it lasted until I could afford to buy more."

As times were hard, Ms Duncan gradually came up with more ways of making savings before deciding to share her knowledge with a wider audience.

When writing the book, she called on family and friends for their input and received lots of useful advice.

She said: "Having no money is a harrowing experience and people need support to help them through.

"This book is about inspiring, motivating and uplifting despondent people. My wish is for readers to start with an open mind and be prepared to finish with a different way of thinking.

"It includes some unusual tips you wouldn't get from a financial adviser but hopefully people find them useful."

Ms Duncan has been active in her community for many years and won a Southwark Culture Award in 2007.

This was in recognition of her work in primary schools helping to promote a positive body image among young children.

She has also been nominated a Beffta (Black Entertainment Fashion Television & Arts) award 2011 as best spoken word poet/a

Ms Duncan performs under name Lyrical Healing and has p at venues including The 1 Festival Hall, Ministry of Soun the Houses of Parliament.

Ms Duncan will be off her book at half price – at £4 throughout October.

Winsome Duncan's top tips:

● Save money on costly contract mobile phone voicemails by diverting them to a pay as you go number with free voicemail.

● In Caribbean cultures, it is traditional at parties to take some leftover food back home

BBC WM Interview, 8pm Sun

BBC RADIO LONDON

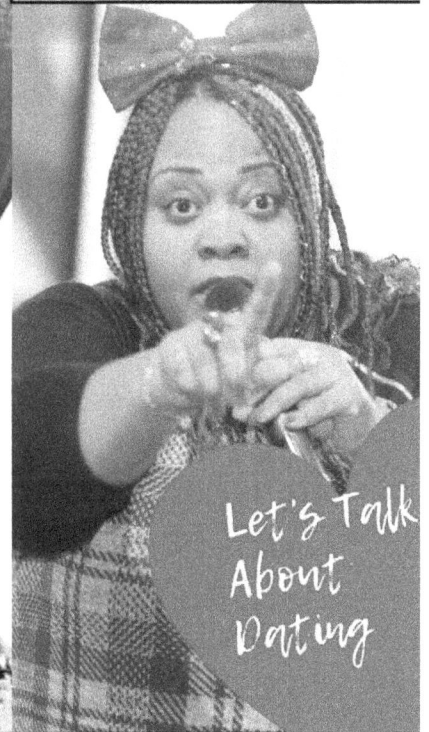

WEDS 22ND APRIL, 8:30PM

Let's Talk About Dating

DON'T MISS IT!

Just Market It

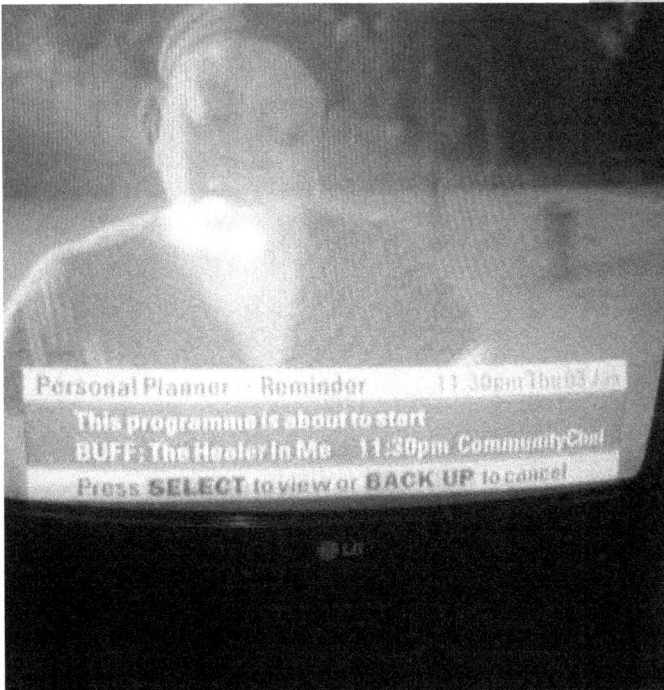

Just Market It

Press Life

"We have to rebalance that current deficit. It cannot be right," Arnold said. "It is just not good enough that currently only four per cent of books reflect the beautiful diversity of our city and our country."

PASSIONATE: Winsome Duncan

The inclusion of two guest authors – Winsome Duncan and James Okoro – in this year's programme drove this point home and gave the children the opportunity to ask an author their burning questions about the book-writing process.

Duncan galvanised the young audience with her enthusiasm about words and writing and her call to action for those in the room to write their own stories, be creative, original and follow guidelines.

Okoro challenged the children to an impromptu spelling test and showcased his books, including *Beetle Reich* and *The Scruffapillar*, to the delight of the young readers.

VOICE

News Sport Lifestyle Entertainment Faith Opinion Video Publications Jobs More   SUBSCRIBE

Search Results for 'WINSOME DUNCAN '

UK NEWS
Tributes flood in to 'inspirational' Barbara Campbell

UK NEWS
Meet the winners of our annual Made By History essay writing competition

BUSINESS
Voice Business Fair proves power of black business

BOOKS
Decade of dating summed up in a handy book

Helping authors fulfil their destiny

Winsome Duncan has been inspired by books since she was a youngster – and now, as part of Peaches Publications, she gives aspiring writers across the world the tools they need to tell their stories...

ON A MISSION: Winsome Duncan helps aspiring authors realise their dreams

Lifestyle: Talk a bit about what you provide as a service?

Winsome Duncan: At Peaches Publications we work with new writers worldwide to turn into their ideas and concepts into a physical book.

Every author is different, each story has light and shade inside them. Some are traumatic like kidnap, sexual abuse, gambling addiction, incest, alcoholism, manslaughter, domestic violence and body dysmorphia.

Whereas others desire to tell their life story, share poetry written 20 years ago, write a book about their passion for God, share sci-fi fiction stories, and Jamaican fables.

Dedication is the key because writing a book is a labour of love that has pressure points that can bring you to tears.

Lifestyle: Tell about the Look Like Me challenge?

WD: This is all exclusive and that focuses on telling stories from the black viewpoint. With only four per cent of space roles showcased in children's books, we compiled in October 2019 to set up a GoFundMe campaign and...

change this narrative. During lockdown we worked with 30 black and Asian children aged seven to 12 years, to create a story named The Popcorn House which is about the importance of diversity.

For three months my team and I have set three workshops on Zoom, where we looked at character development, storylines, artistic drawing, creative concepts and storytelling.

L: What are some of your own favourite books?

WD: Crystal Swain-Bates. Crystal is a bestselling children's author who is featured in...

Youngsters hit screen to tell stories of Our Black History Heroes

---

Entertainment

Decade of dating summed up in a handy book

Winsome Duncan's had disasters and delights in romance – and now she reveals all her tips

BY JOEL CAMPBELL

LET'S BE honest, online dating can be a minefield – but like it or not, it's become a serious option for the millions who have exhausted every other avenue to find love.

Winsome Duncan, *inset*, is no exception to the game and it's been an decade trying to lure...

dating started in 1994, I was motivated by my tears of frustration and continual disappointment of meeting dates who were somehow broken in their form.

I was accused of being a serial dater and I was left depressed and crying for a week and it prompted me to think about why I left...

tic and a journey about self-discovery.

It is important for me to highlight safety issues for those who are new to online dating and to provide tools for people who have been unsuccessful in communicating online.

Lifestyle: You detail some sketchy dalliances, even one with a...

purpose because the subject of finding love can be so, well, not funny?

WD: I have to laugh at my pain, it keeps me sane.

I am a joker by nature and when I wrote this book, I wanted to show readers the light and shade of the dating culture.

I think my descriptions are so decorative that one would have to share some chuckles over a glass of red wine.

Lifestyle: Who has a harder time, men or women, and who...

is higher. Since the book's release, men have spoken to me more than females about heartaches or player ways in online dating.

This book is medicine for a heartbreak and benefits both sexes as it has universal appeal, men and women can use the 65 rules that are listed.

Lifestyle: What's next for you on the literary front?

WD: I am ex-

uals for the book in YouTube spoofs and our dating chat show LoveNet.

He Loves Me Not is available now on all good book-selling platforms.

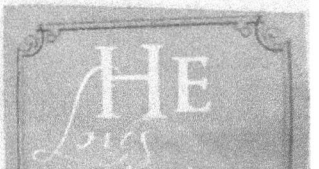

"Once you figure out your purpose, you will never have to work another day in your life."

Winsome Duncan

The Rose Formula

The essence of this book is weaved around the tapestry of The ROSE Formula. Whichever aspect of your marketing campaign you are approaching always keep these four pillars at the forefront of your mind.

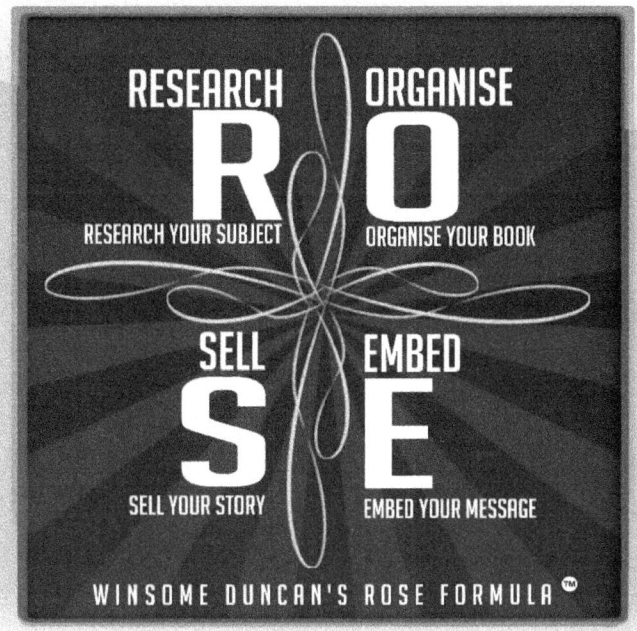

Research

Become an investigator. You will ALWAYS find me looking on YouTube and Amazon for hot new trends, online courses, the latest books, observing book covers, checking their rankings, and seeing who published them. You must see who your competitors are and improve on their weaknesses. Know your subject matter and your story inside out. Be so great that they cannot ignore you.

Organise

Get your book in order; if you know deep down in your heart that you can improve on the interior or exterior or fix that spelling error, then go for it. Let your book be the best representation it can be for the public. Do not play in the realms of mediocrity and 'Oh It Will Be Okay Street'. Step into your greatness and get your book published. Otherwise, it will always haunt you. Once you know your book is the bomb.com, then you can transcend into the higher echelon of organising a savvy, book-marketing campaign.

Sell

People buy into you. First impressions count. I have had to learn the art of selling without selling, if you understand what I mean. Once you tap into your prospects' desires and needs, you should be able to get them to purchase products from you. Always ask yourself: "What is in it for them? How will they feel after they have brought your product or service?" Share with them the benefit of the feature and get them to use their imagination to see into the future; how they can be a better person after their interaction with you.

Embed

Your book message is prevalent when embedding your story into the minds of your readers and consumers. Learn to hone your skill to carefully craft an effective, dynamic message that will be remembered for years to come. You must seed your core message into the mind of your buyers and make them line up to give you, their money. There is a skill to this, and my best advice would be to watch copy editing tutorials on YouTube and learn persuasive language.

Core Message

As an author you need to have a core message about your brand that you take with you to interviews, press releases, television, and radio. Your core message is something you want to embed into your audience mind. For Peaches Publications my core message is 'we publish books' or 'building book legacies'. I say these on repeat. Your message should not be longer than a phase or one sentence. Go ahead and create your Core message below.

Write a one sentence core message:

_____

_____

Foundation Steps to Passive Income

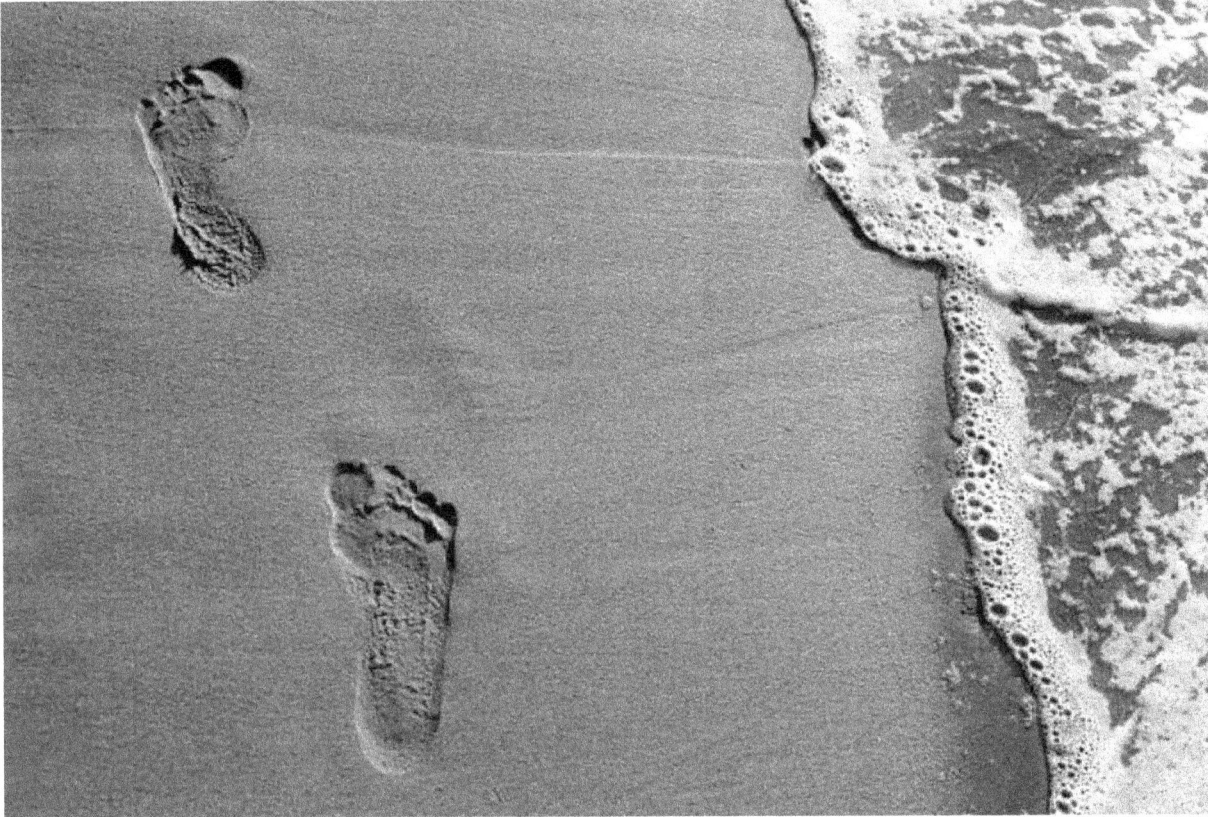

There is a process to everything in life. A marketing campaign is no different; one must be diligent in one's approach when it comes to promotional building blocks of learning what you do not know. How do you eat an elephant? One bite at a time. It is important for you to recognise the areas in which you need support; for example, if you are confident in public speaking but not confident in copywriting, then you need to do one of two things. Go online and learn about copywriting; take a free class on Eventbrite or outsource and get somebody else to do your copywriting for your websites—that includes your keywords from Google planner. Footprints in the sand wash away with time; what you need to create is footprints in cement, as you move forward with your marketing campaign.

We are now going to take a look at the skill sets you are good at, identify the areas in which you can improve and whether you will outsource them or handle them yourself.

Concrete Footprints

The only steps that matter are the footprints left in concrete, for that is where certainty lives, and change takes place.

Write a list of skillsets that you are good at and skillsets that can be outsourced. Be honest in your approach, as this is for your own reference of self-development. Here are my first two entries.

Strong Skillsets	Notes	Outsource (Y/N)
Creativity	Writing books	N
Session planning	Masterclasses & workshops	N
Weak Skillsets		
Website HTML	Hire tech support	Y
Delegation of tasks	Expand the team	Y

Marketing Definition

Marketing is defined by the American Marketing Association as:

the activity, set of institutions, and processes for creating, communicating, delivering, and exchanging offerings that have value for customers, clients, partners, and society at large". Wikipedia

Noun: The definition of marketing is the act and process of buying and selling. An example of marketing is creating advertisements for a product. Your Dictionary definition and usage example.

Advertising and Promotional Definition

Advertising is defined by the Oxford Dictionary as:

Noun

The activity of profession of producing advertisements for commercial products of services.
"an advertising agency"

Advertisements collectively
"despite being instructed to take the signs down, he says he has no intention of removing the advertising"

Source: https://languages.oup.com/google-dictionary-en/

Promotion is defined as:

noun

1. Activity that supports or encourages a cause, venture, or aim.
   "the promotion of cultural and racial diversity"

2. The publicizing of a product, organization, or venture so as to increase sales or public awareness.
   "a sales promotion company"

Source: https://languages.oup.com/google-dictionary-en/

Amazon Author Central

An Amazon Author Central page is a foundation brick when using Kindle Direct Publishing (KDP). So why is this an oversight in so many of my masterclasses? Authors start spluttering and wiggling in their chairs, and they try to justify why this section is not completed. Cut the excuses and let us get real; this is a free tool for you to use and commercially exploit. This is a gem and worth the whole cost of this book. Get your brand right and update. The main four features at Amazon Author Central are:

Profile Picture – Use a professional picture; please, *no* selfies. If you are on a budget, buy a ring light and use a high quality 2K or 4K phone. You can check out my shop page on www.bookconfidencecoach.com for my personal light ring recommendation.

Biography – Here is an opportunity for you to list all your areas of expertise and sell yourself. Be sure to update your biography every six months to a year. Ensure you include your website but not your email or telephone number.

Videos – This is a great space to features interviews, book trailers and testimonials.

Pictures – You can upload pictures of your launch, 3D book promotions or newspaper clippings here.

Multiple Books: If you have written more than a few books, be sure that you have linked all your formats to your Amazon Author Central page; for example, paperback, Kindle, hardback, and audio.

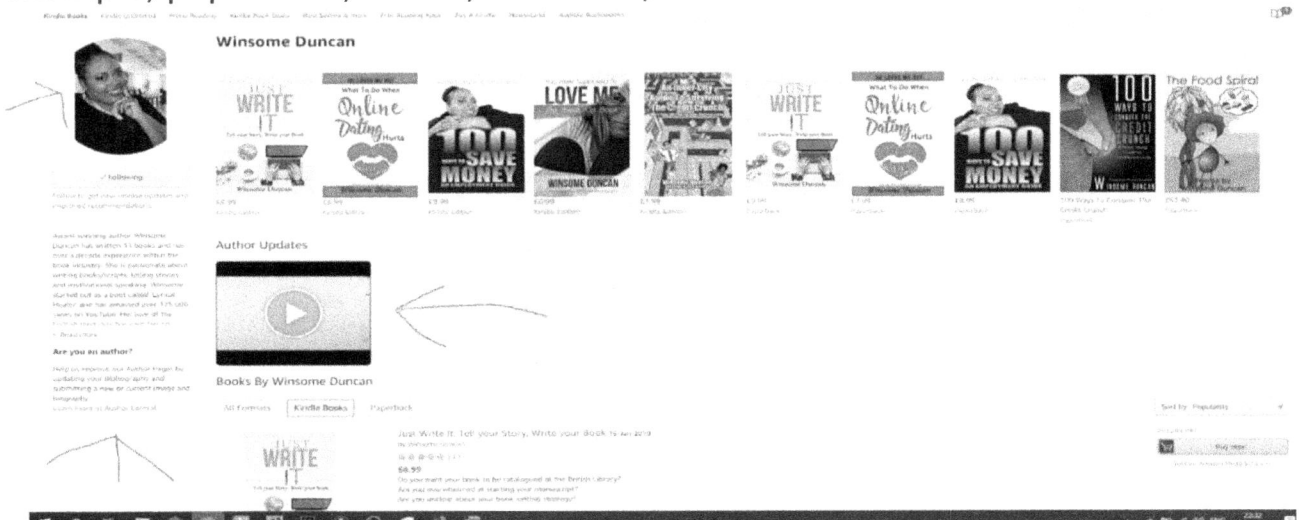

Just Market It

Sadly, for Rapper Stormzy, Merky Books publishing have not seen the relevance of him signing up to Amazon Author Central. This is upsetting to me because he is one the rare Black publishers in the UK. Below is a prime example of what *not* to do on your Amazon Central page. It annoys me seeing this, especially as I did a post and tagged in Merky Books.

Do they not care? It looks unprofessional; think about all the traffic that goes to this page, most of whom have never heard of this talented young man. Now they have missed an opportunity to know and google him for further research and, more importantly, purchase his books. It is such a wasted opportunity. If you know Stormzy or his circle, I plead with you to inform them. Even his co-author Jude Yawson has set up his profile, so why not tell Stormzy to do the same? I do not understand, how irritating.

Stormzy

+ Follow

Follow to get new release updates and improved recommendations

Customers Also Bought Items By

Derek Owusu   Charlamagne Tha God

Neil Martinez-Belkin   Dan Hancox

Rick Ross   Jevan Pradas

£4.99
Kindle Edition

Books By Stormzy

All Formats | Kindle Books | Audiobooks | Hardcover | Paperback

Rise Up: The #Merky Story So Far 01-Nov-2018
by Stormzy
⭐⭐⭐⭐☆ (101)
£4.99 £10.99
A 2018 BOOK OF THE YEAR

'An inspirational must-read.' *Evening Standard*
˅ Read more

Other Formats: Audible Audiobooks , Hardcover , Paperback

The Author Brand Story

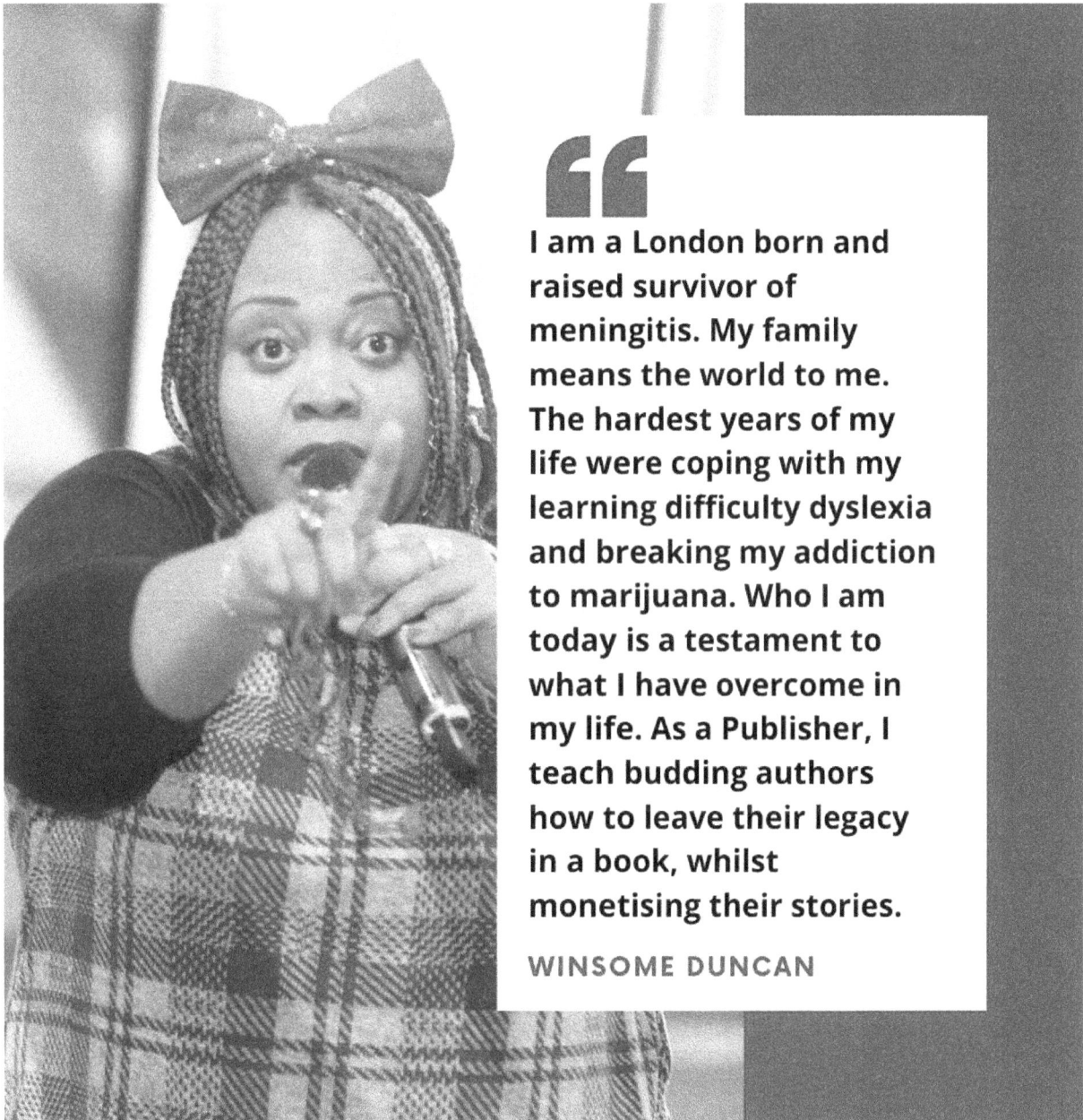

> **I am a London born and raised survivor of meningitis. My family means the world to me. The hardest years of my life were coping with my learning difficulty dyslexia and breaking my addiction to marijuana. Who I am today is a testament to what I have overcome in my life. As a Publisher, I teach budding authors how to leave their legacy in a book, whilst monetising their stories.**
>
> WINSOME DUNCAN

One-sentence life story: I am a survivor who overcame addiction and is dyslexic; today, I teach budding authors to tell their stories.

Write the story of your entire life in one sentence:

_____

_____

_____

Just Market It

A brand story is concise and gets straight to the point. The purpose of this story is to give your audience an insight into your human and vulnerable side. It should be no more than fifty words, and your picture needs to be attached to it. This should be used in your presentations, in your social media and as part of your profile-building persona.

Create your brand story of 50 words or less here:

Edit your brand story of 50 words or less here:

Six Book Formats

Write the vision down and make it plain if you are serious about opening up ALL streams of income for your book, then you need to be constantly working towards creating as many formats of your books as possible for sale. To leverage your income, what are the six formats in which you can monetise your books? I have given you the first answer for free because I am generous like that. Now be creative and think; do not cheat and turn the page because you will be doing yourself a disservice.

"Quitters never win; winners never quit" – Lisa Nichols

1 Paperback

2_____

3_____

4_____

5_____

6_____

"Learn to sell ice to Eskimos."

Winsome Duncan

Six Book Formats

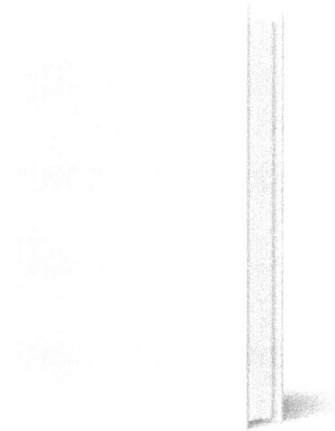

Six Ways to Monetise Your Book

How many out of six did you get? Be honest, list your number here:
_____

It is vital to pursue the majority – if not all – of these book formats to set yourself apart from other authors. Go the extra mile. Too many authors think way too small for my liking and say, 'I do not have the money yet' or, 'I have not budgeted for this'. Every day, I hear all kinds of excuses, blockages, and obstacles on the phone and in person. Sometimes these excuses frustrate me, to be honest, but then I remember experience is the kindest teacher and the following three things spring to mind:

1. I do not control or run the universe.
2. When authors make excuses, they get to keep them.
3. This is their book journey, not mine, I cannot desire to write or sell an authors' book more than them.
4. Let go and let God.

That was a tough pill to swallow because I used to be offended at the fact that authors no longer wanted my help, or they choose to go at a slower pace, or they fell off the face of the planet, never to be seen again even though they paid for services. I felt like somehow, I was not doing my job properly because they were not copying the breakneck speeds I was going at. However, what I learnt was to let go and let God and send them on their merry way with smiles and best wishes. Everything is working for the good of mankind, and I am just a small part of their journey.

So here we are talking about money again, does it scare you? Are you feeling uncomfortable? Does the thought of expanding your book portfolio take you out of your comfort zone? If yes, then that is amazing. Stepping up to the bar and selling more books takes guts and effort. Let us look at what are the best options for you to start diversifying your income streams.

Just Market It

1. Paperback

Paperback books are the most common books in production and are generally cost-effective in their price. The best option for you to select is 'print on demand', also known as 'POD'. You can opt to send books to Amazon and become a marketplace seller, but I only advise that for hardback editions.

2. CD books

CD books are still available, but they are old school and are bulky. Readers often opt for books they can hear on Audible or on YouTube. If you would like to do a CD book, I would suggest a small number to test the market, and the rest of the recording should be uploaded onto Audible.

3. eBooks

eBooks are leading the way and are increasing in popularity every day. I am a traditionalist, so to me, they will never replace the good old paperback. What I love about eBooks, though, is that you earn more of the profit on Kindle with a 70% to 30% ratio in your favour. You must make sure the formatting is correct for your eBooks; otherwise, you will get complaints and low ratings. In general, eBooks should be half the cost of a normal paperback as there are no delivery or printing cost.

4. Hardback

Hardback books are so special because they can be a collector's item or a luxury edition. The beauty about selling hardbacks is not only is it another income stream, but you can sell them for double the price or triple the price because it is a limited edition and readers like collector items.

5. Audio Books

Audio books are extremely popular for busy people and professionals who like to multitask. It helps the listener connect with you personally and build a great rapport with you. We recommend you use Lily Naadu Mensah's services when it comes to recording your books, see next page for details.

6. Personalised USB sticks

Brand Consultant Lily Naadu Mensah is a great example of this gift idea. I purchased her book and received a beautiful branded red package which included her paperback book, CD and USB stick with an MP3 version of her book. It gave me various ways to access her book, and her USB stick was personalised. Come on now, up your book business game!

Lily Naadu Mensah beautifully records audio books and uploads them onto Audible for you, please contact Lily and quote '**QUIRKY**' when you email her here: lily@lilymensah.com.

"Selling a book is a hustle n flow."

Winsome Duncan

Look Inside Feature

The 'Look Inside' feature is a fantastic free tool given to you by Amazon to help you sell more books to your prospective readers. You have to remember that Amazon has millions of buyers on their sites looking for what you are offering, so it is important to take advantage of all these features. If you upload your Kindle book to Amazon, the 'Look Inside' feature will come a lot quicker than if it is in paperback when it can take up to fourteen days for your paperback 'Look Inside' feature to arrive. I want you to understand why it is so vital for you as an author to make sure that you know as much information as possible moving forward.

You need to include these features to get your book to be the best that it can be. Be sure to make sure that the typeset is done correctly and that the table of contents page looks good. If your book is small, a children's picture book of, say, about thirty pages, they probably will only show the first few pages, and you might not get to the images inside because it is a small book so just be mindful of that. The bigger the book, the more 'Look Inside' feature they will show, so make sure your book is neat and tidy for your prospective buyer to purchase and your description opening includes catchy sentences. This is crucial in the process of becoming a bestselling author.

Pre-order

I love Pre-order on Amazon Kindle.

Again, this is a free tool that offers you an opportunity to pre-sell the Kindle edition of your book prior to it being available to the public and before your launch. It is so exciting because your new title this has the potential of getting you a number one slot on Kindle as soon as your book is released. If you can drum up enough pre-sales in the ninety days or less, your book can hit the number one spot, but it takes work.

Be warned that Amazon gives you a time limit regarding the uploading of your final manuscript. For example, if your manuscript is to be launched on the 10th of December, Amazon will notify you one week beforehand and they will say you must upload your final manuscript. In this case it would be the 3rd December, for your final copy of your book that needs to be submitted. Unfortunately, if your manuscript is not submitted and remains incomplete, then Amazon will ban you from using their Pre-order service for a whole year. I know this from personal experience. I did not have my book ready, and for a whole year, all I could do was just upload straight away and could not use this facility.

You will have two options when doing your Pre-order. They will ask you, 'Is your book ready now?' Select 'yes it is the final version' or 'no I am going to upload it later', then you need to make sure that you upload that book before midnight on the 3rd of December. This is very key to the process. When you have the link, send it out to all your social media platforms as soon as it goes live—it normally takes 24 to 72 hours, but usually, in 24 hours, it will go live. This is also a great way to keep to deadlines and targets: once you put a date out there, you must stick to it.

Get Organised and Mobilise

To write your book, you must be organised, diligent and focused. Editing takes commitment, energy, and time. Once your book is written, you need to create a plan to get it out to the mass market.

Many people have small book dreams or goals, and they do not understand the depth of their creativity and how they can increase their income streams with one book in their hand. Being organised means keeping a diary, noting relevant dates, sticking to appointments and being reliable. Make sure that you respond back to customer or client queries in a timely fashion. When you can create trust between your fans and your readership, it will be an amazing job moving forward.

Army camps mobilise their troops before they go out onto the battlefield. You are going onto the book battlefield so you need to be fully prepared for war as you step into the competitive world of literature. Be bold and leave your message, leave your mark, so it is important that you understand the significance of what I say here. The story that you have to tell needs to grow legs internationally; it is no good putting some flimsy pictures on Instagram and hoping and praying that your book sells. You need to have a clear, definitive plan as to where you are going with this project. You must create your book plan.

Creative Marketing Budget

Being broke is a state of mind. Is your glass of life half-empty or half-full? Many people put in offers or approach me to work with them but later say, 'Oh, I cannot do it because X' or, 'I do not have the funds'.

Writing is free of charge.

The only cost to write in is your time, and you know time is a precious commodity. When you write, you are telling your story your intellect; what it is that you know. You need to *invest* in your book. Period! You need to view your book as a book business; you must now get focused, and even if you do not have much money, make the money that you do have stretch—and make it stretch far and wide.

A creative budget is what you will spend on your marketing campaigns, as a double entendre it also means being creative on a tight budget. If you are not investing in your marketing campaign, you are not serious about earning money back on your book. You need to take this seriously and start to map out your budget for your book. The next table is a budget for you to think about some ideas on how you are going to spend the money that you earn—not paying bills but investing it into your book business. Your budget should be £500 to £2,000 when starting this journey. I have left the rest of the boxes blank so that you can fill them in if you think of anything else you want to add. This is a basic budget plan. I spend a lot more on my marketing budget.

May people create a Go Fund Me page to support different elements of their dreams. Family and friends are always willing to support you when you are bold enough to step forward and create the life you want. I have created a YouTube video called: How to Run a Successful Go Fund Me Campaign.

You can Google it for view it here:
http://www.peachespublications.co.uk/go-fund-me.html

Creative Marketing Budget

Items	Cost
Book stock (100)	£345
Postage & package	£225
Graphic design for branding	£350
Amazon advertising	£200
Press distribution	£150
Press Pack	£149
Relaunch	£300
Guest performance	£100
	£
	£
Total	£1,819

Blank Creative Marketing Budget

Items	Cost
Book stock (100)	£
Postage & package	£
Graphic design for branding	£
Amazon advertising	£
Press distribution	£
Press Pack	£
Relaunch	£
Guest performance	£
	£
	£
	£
	£
	£
	£
Total	£

Free ISBNs vs Paid ISBNs

What does ISBN stand for?

An ISBN is your unique identity number to you and your book or your product. No one else shares this, and in order to trade on Amazon, you will need an ISBN number and a barcode creator to add to your product.

I use both free and paid ISBNs for different reasons: Amazon's ISBNs are free, but that means you cannot put in your publisher's details and it will show up on the listing as 'independent publisher' which looks unprofessional. This means basically that you have self-published your book. This route (self-publishing) can have some stigma attached to it. I use free Amazon ISBN for journals and colouring books. I use paid ISBN from Nielsen's Bookdata for books published under my name and company Peaches Publications or Look Like Me Book Challenge. The benefit of having Nelson's book data barcode ISBN is that you will get your book listed on Waterstones website, and it will be available to an expanded market for distribution. This means that you can approach Waterstones and ask them to stock your book in their shops across the UK. However, you do need to be selling several hundreds of your books each month over a steady period of time for them to seriously consider you. They are quite strict with hybrid publishers and self-publishers. To be honest self-publishers hardly get our books listed due to institutionalised snobbery and white fat cat syndrome.

Answer: It simply means 'international standard barcode number'.

Upgrade Your Mindset

Look carefully at the picture below and tell me what do you see below?

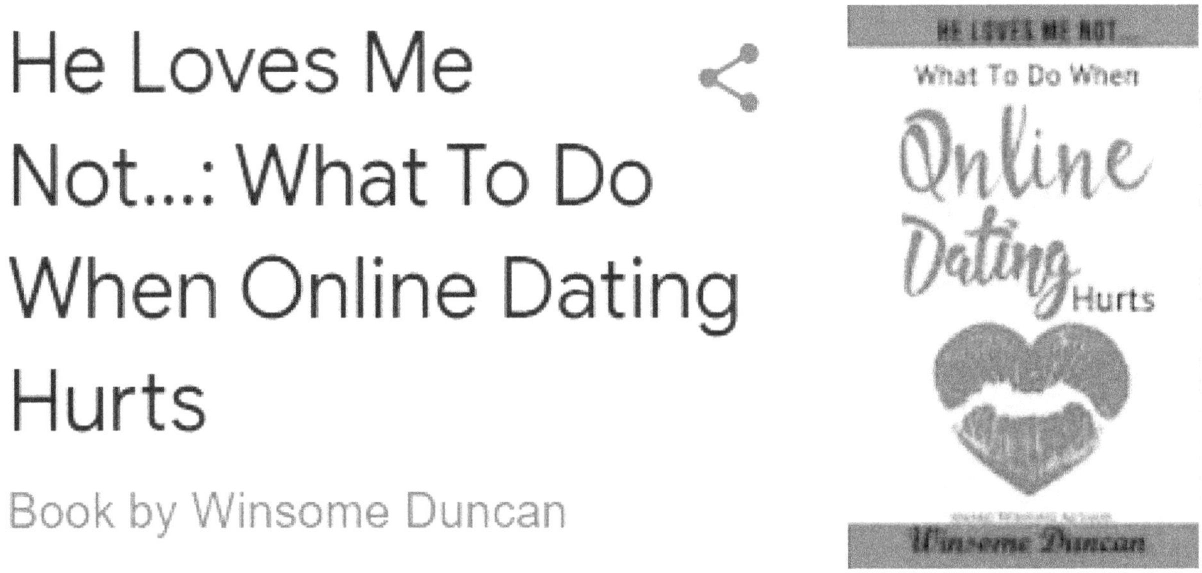

He Loves Me Not...: What To Do When Online Dating Hurts
Book by Winsome Duncan
HE LOVES ME NOT...
What To Do When
Online
Dating
Hurts
Winsome Duncan

Just Market It

If you are looking at this product and you only see a book, then you are thinking in one-dimensional terms. This is not just a book; this is a trilogy boxset; this is a dating show; this is a TV series. There is this famous saying I quoted at the start: "The mind is like a parachute - it works best when open" by Frank Zappa . You have to expand the vision for your book if you want to start up a book business. It is possible if you only believe. That you are a visionary. This is also an opportunity to maximise your income. My recommendation is always that you get your books in the format of:

- Paperback
- Audio book
- Hardback

Paperback

Paperback books will always be much cheaper than hardback books. You must make sure that your price is competitive and that you do not outprice yourself in your market. It is better to sell large numbers of low-price products than small amounts of high-priced products, in my opinion. Amazon books are really cost-effective; however, if you are looking for a more premium product, I suggest that you publish your books independently in order to increase the paper weight of your book page and the card weight of your exterior book jacket. Please note that Amazon currently does not provide a print on demand service for hardback books.

Audio book

Audio books are a great way of getting your message out to your readers who like to listen to books rather than read. These are normally busy Entrepreneurs, so it is good to cater to their market. Also, if you have a children's book, then it is a great idea for you to record that and to upload it onto Audible. There is a link at the end of the book to the website for you to view.

Hardback

Investing in a hardback edition to your book is a great way of expanding your income streams. You can market this product as a luxury limited-edition product. What is exciting about hardbacks is that they are sturdier, they last longer, and they have a higher price point. It would be remiss of me to not reiterate the benefits of a hardback edition of your book, which you can order from a publisher, or you can simply go online and use a print-on-demand company.

You also need to have your book on all online platforms like iBooks or Google Books. Kobo makes it available to different platforms so that you can have different streams of income and not just rely on Amazon. When Amazon is ready, they can say to you, they reserve the right not to publish your book and block your title. Unfortunately, they did so with my journal 'The Day the Earth Stopped.'

"There is a sound to selling; it is called ching-ching."

Winsome Duncan

Benefits of Word of Mouth

Obtaining recommendations via word of mouth is the most important way to get business to you fast. If someone has had a good experience with your book and it has transformed their lives or inspired them, their recommendation will not only cause you to sell more of your books, but it could potentially get you to number one on the bestsellers list.

You can upsell your products and services to your medium to high price points. Always be professional in your approach to your books. If someone pays you, send the book out within one to two days.

When I send books internationally to be reviewed by influencers, I make a lost on the postage, however I understand the value of placing my book in front of thousands of people who are not in my network yet. Be inspired in your customer service, speed is the best option. Pre-order book sales are the exception and customers should expect a waiting period of anticipation.

You can begin to hone your presentation and speaking skills at home, and that way, you can get a captivated audience that will be falling over themselves to purchase your books and services. If you go online to Eventbrite you can book free and paid training to help you boost your confidence, increase your vocal projection, learn basic book-keeping and invoices. I am a motivational speaker and I have learned how to engage an audience.

Social Media Accounts

The first thing I would like to say here is you really need to take time out and take a course on leveraging your social media platforms. This is an extremely specific task and cannot be covered in its entirety in this book. This is a mammoth task within itself to manage your social media accounts. The different platforms offer different things; for example, Instagram is about pictures while Facebook is about stories and family. To begin to unpack, managing your social media accounts is a huge task going forward, and you must do your due diligence and research what is the best one for you. I am just going to give you a brief insight into what I believe could help you if you are a beginner on this journey.

be consistent in posting online;
offer value;
offer free content;
engage with your fanbase by responding to comments and liking their posts;
understand what each social media site does and how it can benefit your book topic;
invest in some social media training;
be clear in the message that you are delivering.

There are so many different social media networks out there. I am just going to tell you what works for me and what I have used, and then you can decide where you want to go:

- YouTube
- Facebook
- Twitter
- Instagram
- LinkedIn

Just Market It

Out of the ones listed above, I would say my Instagram receives the most feedback and engagement. My Facebook receives the second-highest feedback. Owing to time constraints, I find it difficult to connect with everyone, it is not particularly healthy either when you own several businesses to try and be everywhere.

The majority of marketing and engagements on my social media will be outsourced for the future. Simply because I do not have the capacity to keep up with everything without being constantly stressed or tired. It is important for me and my business to go to the next level by automating my services and making sure that I have a strong team beside me to help my business to grow and expand.

There comes a time when you must hand over the reins and get support. Robert Kiyosaki talks about this in his book *Rich Dad Poor Dad.* He says, "You must work on your and not in your business."

I am not doing this as much as I should business. His words have always stayed with me, and this is what I am striving to do now.

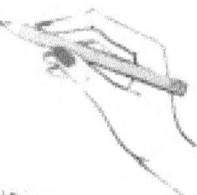

Social Media Checklist

It is important to spread the word about your book. You need to get comfortable promoting your book on social media. Remember, learn what you do not know on YouTube or outsource this to a marketing company. However, be mindful not to get exploited as their rates are high. The checklist below tells you what each social media platform does. You must tick off once you have joined. I have left some blank spaces for you to add other social media sites that are not listed below.

Social Media	Description	Joined
Facebook	Facebook is great for staying connected to family and friends and sharing life events. They only expose your post to 10% or less of your friends list. If you want the message of your book to get out to the market, you need to pay them for advertising.	
Twitter	Twitter is a concise message platform. Just like your mobile, it allows only 140 characters per message. You need to make sure that your post is succinct and precise. It is also a great place to create or share quotes. If you add a picture or a link, you do not use up any of your 140-character allocation. It is common for abbreviations to be use on here.	
LinkedIn	LinkedIn is normally used for businesspeople, Entrepreneurs and companies wanting to hire staff. If you run your own business and employ people, this is a good site for you to be on because of the professional contacts that are available.	

Just Market It

Snapchat	Snapchats are short bursts of videos or text which you can animate and add several different filters or effects to. You then share these online. I like the beauty effect.	
Instagram	This is mainly for pretty pictures and has a 24-hour story feed. You can record up to one minute of content.	
IGTV	More recently, Instagram have introduced IGTV, where you can post content for up to one hour. This is great for workshop style interaction.	
YouTube	YouTube is the second biggest search engine in the world. This is a great opportunity for you to create your own television channel and potentially reach millions. Remember, advertising is cheaper on this platform because it is so vast.	
Pinterest	This is a great site for creating vision boards for the future.	
24 Hour stories	Across most platforms there is a useful feature called 24 hours stories. You should use this for daily content, promotions, and animated video uploads.	

Remember, social media is forever changing and adding new things to the mix. Be sure to stay up to date with the trends. This list shows some of the resources I use; however, there are loads more you can add.

The Smoke and Mirror Illusion

The book industry is about the illusion of being bigger than what you really are. So many times, I hear authors brag about how many thousands of books they have sold, which became number-one bestsellers. Verbally, they sound like an authority in their field. When I look online at the Amazon sales ranking, their book chart in the thousands; they are definitely not in the bestseller Top 100. What that tells me is that their book is not selling as much as they are making it out to be. However, there might have been a time where for an hour or two, they hit the hotspot or maybe even a day. This is the wave you must ride upon in your journey because as soon as you get any accolades online, it shows the world what you have achieved.

This is key to creating the image of how successful your book is. Let me give you an example:

I was working on a book launch and we did Pre-orders on Kindle downloads, although the book would not be out for another couple of weeks. What was exciting about this was that three people Pre-ordered the book online, and when I looked in the bestseller rank, I noticed that the book was at number 25! This is amazing considering that, out of the billions of books on Amazon, this one hit 25! This was a great opportunity for the author to promote the book by saying, for example. "Look, I am in the top 25!" The secret to this is going to be written in my last entry at the back of the book called 'How to Become a Bestseller on Amazon'.

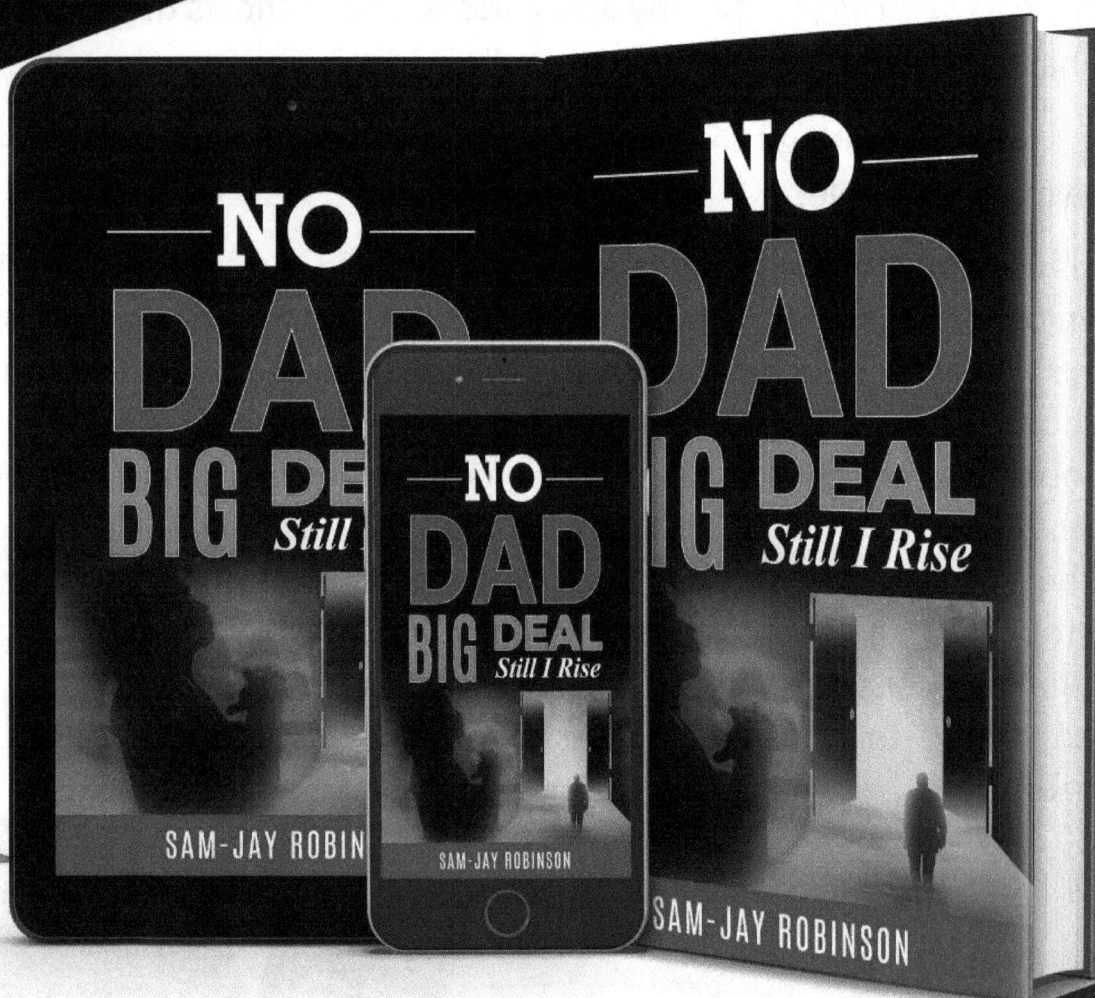

JUST MARKET IT

Starting A Book Business

There is a difference between starting a book business and selling your book as an author. If you are serious about diversifying your revenue, then really you need to refer to your books as a 'book business'. This takes courage, commitment, focus and dedication.

You will begin to learn the skills needed to hit your first target of 300 sales of your book. In a book's lifetime, 300 copies are normally its peak sale. However, you must aim to supersede that and make sure that you can understand the process of how to leverage your income from your book; from it being a low-price product to it being monetised in different ways.

We will go over this in more detail when we talk about how to separate your services and your products and how to maximise and leverage them. This is important, you need to learn what you do not know, and you must be willing to step out of your comfort zone when starting a book business.

Everything that I have learned is either through my own mental abilities or by researching on YouTube or by Googling it. I often go online to find out things that I do not know; things that I am not 100% versed on, I make sure I learn constantly. Remember, we have got academic doctorial information online for fast learning, so with this in mind, be confident that you too can earn an extra income from your book.

The following page is an A4 micro business plan for your book business. The way I see it, if you cannot spend the time to write down on one piece of paper your vision for your book business and how you should implement these tasks, then maybe it is not the right time for you to market your book. Remember HMRC views any additional income as sole trader earnings. Therefore, Amazon asks all my clients in their Amazon Tax Interview if they have a Unique Tax Reference number. If you do not, you must pay them 30% of your royalties' earnings to cover your tax shortfall. Be very aware of your legal responsibilities.

Micro Business Plan

Micro Book Business Plan

Company/Author Name

Company Description

Target Market

Staffing

Competitors and Research

Income Streams

S.W.O.T.

Strengths	Opportunities
Weaknesses	Threats

Products and Services

Start-up Costs

Identifying your Marketer Avatars

Having worked with authors for more than a decade, I have identified and created the top four Marketer Avatars that I encounter regularly. Inevitably, you will fit into one of these Avatars, which will help you to understand the way in which you approach the marketing and advertising of your book and will provide ways you can improve. Take a close look at the descriptions on the next page and write the name of your Avatar below.

My Primary Marketer Avatar is: _____

Please list three traits of your avatar:

1_____

2_____

3_____

My Secondary Marketer Avatar is: _____

Please list three traits of your avatar:

1_____

2_____

3_____

Confused Marketer

> Ugh!
> I am not technological

??? ? ??

www.bookconfidencecoach.com

The confused marketer will always be three steps behind because turning on a laptop freaks them out. They need to get a grip on reality and hire an expert to help them or take some online training courses and overcome their fear.

-------- Winsome Duncan --------

Newbie Marketer

> Let me research **how to sell** more books

www.bookconfidencecoach.com

The newbie marketer is fresh-faced and optimistic at the thought of learning something new. They are not intimidated by the unknown and would benefit from writing down a plan of what marketing areas they would like to learn first.

-------- Winsome Duncan --------

Self-Taught Marketer

Let me check my Book Royalties

www.bookconfidencecoach.com

The self-taught marketer is a dapper don! They think fast on their feet and crave knowledge to expand their marketing know-how. To their credit, everything they have learned has been through sheer grit and determination. They would benefit from being mentored by a guru genius.

-------- Winsome Duncan --------

Guru Marketer

I do this in my sleep

www.bookconfidencecoach.com

The guru marketer has a degree in marketing and understands the principles of advertising. They earn six figures each year and understand value propositions and customer avatars. They take the time to learn new apps and follow the latest trends.

-------- Winsome Duncan --------

Identifying your Target Customer

When you market your book, even when the subject matter is an autobiography or memoir, you must always have the reader in mind. Remember they are your end-user, a buyer, a prospect, or a potential client. You must be clear about the narrative you want to get across. Customers are the ones who will purchase your books and anything else you are selling. This means that marketing your books, products and services is not about self-gratification but more about tuning into the experience that you want your reader to have. Here are some real-life examples of authors I have worked with, to help you define what their readership should be.

Target Readership	Book Content
Millennials aged 27 to 33	The author writes about dating online.
Young Black males and educational establishments	The author wanted to raise awareness of mental health issues in young black men.
Overweight people who struggle with their health. Medical Professionals.	The author shares healthy Caribbean recipes to reduce obesity, strokes, and heart attacks.
Helping families to become financially literate	The author writes a book about budgeting and improving your finances.

Now it is time to write down your targeted reader's profile. The purpose of this task is to know what characteristics your readers have and how you can place your book in front of them and get onto the Amazon 100 bestsellers list. To build a well-rounded profile, you must include:

Just Market It

- Race
- Class
- Age
- Demographics
- Marital status
- Social meet-ups
- Magazines or newspapers they read
- Where they shop for food and clothes
- How many children do they have?

It might also help you to think carefully about the processes that brought you to *this* book. Why did you purchase the *JUST MARKET IT* workbook? What need or purpose does it fulfil? How can it help your book business? Let us begin with you, thinking about the reason why you brought this book, I want you to now create a customer profile of yourself. The idea is for you to get use to understanding who your customers are.

Write your customer profile here based on the information above:

Sample Target Buyer Profile

Rosie is married to Derek. They have two daughters, aged 15 and 19 years old. Rosie's family is middle class. Derek works in a Canary Wharf bank, and they live in Buckinghamshire. Rosie is a Black female aged 43 years and is a stay-at-home mother. She now wants to start a part-time business to counteract being bored at home. In the evenings and some weekends when she is home, Rosie likes to read *Vogue* and *O Magazine,* and her favourite newspaper is *The Sunday Times*.

Rosie makes regular online purchases and shops in organic food stores and supermarkets like: Sainsbury's, Waitrose, and Selfridges. Rosie loves to attend networking events, conferences, seminars, business brunches and weekend spas with her daughters and close friends.

Sample Target Buyer Profile

Marsha is single. She has one son aged 7 years old. Marsha is working class. She is a teacher and lives in Hackney. Marsha is a mixed race female aged 36 years. She wants to increase her passive income to be more financially stable. Marsha sources her news online, via her mobile phone and is computer literate.

Marsha shops in Tesco, Asda and Aldi and makes regular purchases on Amazon and eBay. Marsha loves entrepreneurial pursuits and business events. She relishes Motivational Speakers and is interested in self-development. On her days off she goes on road trips to visit family, friends, and museums.

Your Target Buyer Reader Profile

Your Target Buyer Reader Profile

Primary and Secondary Target Audience

It is important to think about the people who will be the primary customers buying your book. For example, if you wrote a book about the Black holocaust, parties interested in buying this book would be cultural studies students, historians, and university lecturers. Your secondary customer would be family members or friends who want to support you and purchase your book; however, they will probably never read it. Write your family and friends in the secondary readership box.

Primary Readership

Secondary Readership

Just Market It

Guerrilla Marketing

This is a great way to capture headlines and go viral. The purpose of this type of marketing is to think about outlandish ways to get your message to the public. Do you remember the MTV Music Awards in 2010? That is when Lady Gaga wore a real animal flesh meat suit. Go ahead and google it. Now, most people might wonder why she would do that? It was to get attention and get the media to focus on her. She is not a vegan, and she was not trying to save the animals. Sometimes you have to be bold and courageous in sending your message out to the media and, more importantly, be remembered for it.

Below is one of our author's books called *Soul of a Woman*. When I heard the song version of 'Soul of a Woman' by Johnny Gill, I went onto Amazon and this is what came up. What is great about this is that it looks like he is looking at the author, Neusa Catoja. The idea for this would be to get a picture or video endorsement from the artist, which can lead to more sales of my book as well as raise my profile:

If this were my book, I would do the following:

- Send a signed copy to his manager
- Send a signed copy to his agent
- Send a signed copy to his record label **Then I would do the following:**
- Announce on social media that I have gifted Johnny Gill a copy of my book with this picture
- Then I would proceed to tag him on all my accounts
- Then tag his family and friends close to him until he was alerted
- Purchase the song and write a review, mentioning my book title and share it online
- Create online posts with the song
- Dance to the song playing in the background
- Contact Tiffany Haddish Agent as she was in the video

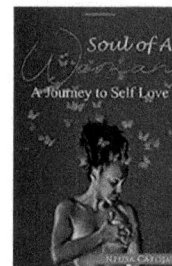

Soul of A Woman: A Journey to Self Love
by Neusa Catoja and Peaches Publications
★★★★★ ~ 10
Paperback
£11¹¹

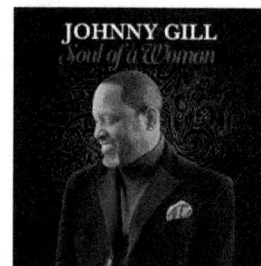

Soul of a Woman
by Johnny Gill
★★★★★ ~ 1
MP3 Download
Listen with Music Unlimited
Or £0.99 to buy MP3 album

Relaunch

If your book is not selling, it could be because of the cover design, which may not appeal to your target audience. You must consider whether the images are correct/suitable/apt and whether the title states or conveys what the book is about.

In the example below, our client, Agnes Cawlyd, went from this to fine-art water colour illustrations. Notice the name change and subtitle change, which all helps to lift her book. Which cover do you prefer now?

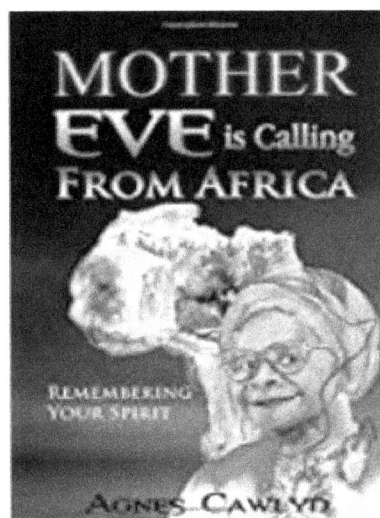

Mailing List

The purpose of a mailing list is to update your fans and supporters concerning what you are doing with your book, and a newsletter would be a great vehicle to inform them of your recent shows on television or radio. This takes organisation and great skill. The easiest way is to integrate an opt-in box on your website which adds fans who agree to sign-up automatically. You do not have to be involved in the process and the process becomes automated.

You would want to grow your mailing list into the thousands in order to have healthy monthly income streams that you could potentially live off or that could help to contribute to the living costs each month. There are several email services for bulk emails available, and this is where your copywriting skills come into play to engage your audience. You should give them previews of your book and some free giveaways. In return, you can request video testimonials and ask for online book reviews.

To get to the top of the Amazon bestselling list, you need a healthy mailing list comprising family, friends and supporters who are interested in your topic and want to read more of your work. This is important because it helps you to create a hub of people who support and celebrate your work.

Are you on Mail Chimp? You receive 1000 FREE email addresses to add to your mailing list and you have several easy template designs. You know that I am a fan of template designs as well, so it is important for me to use this site to stay in contact. This is one of the secrets of getting people to give you book reviews and, on launch day, getting your book into the bestsellers list on Amazon. Make sure that you meet General Data Protection Regulations (GDPR) rules and regulations and register with Information Commissioner's Office (ICO) for a data protection licence to store people's email addresses.

Loss Leaders

The purpose of the loss leader is to get customers into your sales funnel. Once they are there, you can introduce to them to other products and services. It is always best to do a digital product as a loss leader because of the low production cost. Some great loss leaders are templates that customers can use, eBooks and iBooks. Your eBook should be ten to maybe twenty pages long, with nicely designed imagery, and it should tell the 'what' but not necessarily the 'how'. When you share this information, you just want to tease the prospect with something that is of value to them, that can be bought, and then you can move forward and sell other products and services. Research online about the different types of loss leaders offered by competitors; a paragraph from a fiction book could be a loss leader, or an audio segment of your book. Always and get some feedback and online reviews.

Do's and Don'ts of Marketing

Do's

Do test your audience engagement levels

Do have a clear core message when reaching your target audience

Do have some freebies or giveaways to help capture new leads

Do provide value content

Do make sure that your audience finds you trustworthy and honest

Do lots of research, remember you do not know what you do not know

Don't

Don't bombard your audience with the same posts

Don't sell to the wrong market

Don't be afraid to try new things

Don't work with people who are not your potential clients

Don't get stuck in the same old thinking

Don't close the door on mutual benefit opportunities

99 Marketing Ideas for Growth

Choosing the best ways to share your marketing message.

Have fun with this and be sure to get creative. The following list are not exhaustive:

1. Podcasts on iTunes and Spotify
2. Giveaways and competitions
3. Social media shoutouts
4. Book tours & virtual book tours
5. Host online events free and paid
6. Expand your merchandise
7. Book signings
8. Bulk buy libraries of each broughs
9. Raise your visibility
10. Become an expert in your field
11. Become an influencer
12. Become a YouTuber
13. Host events in person
14. Create gift packs and bundles
15. Book hampers
16. Create a showreel
17. Facebook pages
18. Facebook groups
19. Vlogging
20. Blogging
21. 24-hours Instagram interview
22. Speaker engagements
23. Radio
24. Book launch
25. Bulk sales (one to many, not one to one)
26. Brand awareness
27. Media press kit
28. Up to date biography

29. 3D book promo images
30. Zoom meetings
31. Paid Amazon adverts for USA and UK
32. Approach book clubs
33. Greetings cards
34. Fridge magnets
35. Cups
36. Pens
37. Instagram-sponsored adds
38. Word of mouth
39. Guerrilla marketing
40. Television adverts
41. Build a strong mailing list
42. Feature in your local paper or magazine
43. Create a regular newsletter
44. Cold call
45. Follow up on leads
46. Use the six degrees of separation to get past gatekeepers
47. Create business cards
48. Design flyers
49. Offer mini discovery calls
50. Create samples of your products
51. Offer free workshops online
52. Create an online course and duplicate it on multiple platforms
53. Create a tribe of loyal followers
54. Get testimonials
55. Make friends with influencers
56. Tag trends in your social media posts, e.g., #entanglement links to Jada Pinkett Smith story
57. Create an email signature with accolades
58. Sponsor events to get your brand visible
59. Offer discounts for a limited time only
60. Create a lost leader (google if you are unsure)
61. Create letter stickers with your logo

62. Add an Amazon affiliate link to your website
63. Create an app
64. Teach your expertise
65. Invest in your search engine optimisation ranking (SEO)
66. Reward repeat business or clients
67. Create a website (even if it is a free one)
68. Be professional by offering great customer service
69. Attend networking events regularly
70. Create a GoFundMe page for your project
71. Enter award nominations
72. Set up a referral fee on Eventbrite and offer your affiliates a percentage of sales from your booking link
73. Use Google AdWords sense
74. Create partnerships with bosses and local business
75. Use a QR code on your products and services
76. Get a deal on Groupon
77. Be controversial
78. Develop your value, so that word of mouth does your marketing
79. Create a book series
80. Write a follow-up book
81. Write a journal
82. Learn to sell via YouTube videos
83. Listen to your customer's feedback
84. Create a free pdf of your expert skills
85. Research and create an online playlist on how to market your book
86. Establish a room on Clubhouse
87. Identify your audience
88. Create a TV show
89. Create an author brand story
90. Create a catchy hook
91. Make it easy to buy your products and services
92. Learn public speaking principles

93. Think outside mediation
94. Have a professional photoshoot (no selfies)
95. Dangle your carrot
96. Create online readings
97. Create a book trailer
98. Add an additional chapter to your book; change your cover design and call it a second edition
99. Sell your book on eBay

Just Market It

You are invited to book your exclusive spot on our ADVANCED Marketing online course. You will access a six-week online video live with your Number 1 Book Confidence Coach,
Winsome Duncan.

Just Market It

Testimonials

Always ask your client's for testimonials; they can be videos, written statements, via social media or email. This shows your product as credible, once in the public domain. Now I want you to write down five people or clients who you will approach for a testimonial then pick up the phone and get in contact with them today.

1. _____

2. _____

3. _____

4. _____

5. _____

Joanna Oliver
1h · 🌐

Winsome Duncan knows her stuff.
She is one of the most prolific entrepreneurs I know.
She is resilient.
Strong.
Creative and...
....super-talented.

It brings me great pleasure to support this new chapter for Winsome. She has earned it.

Experience is priceless and having worked alongside Winsome for the past six years, I know she has this in bags and then some.

If you want guidance coming from a place of real insight, speak to Winsome...speak to Winsome Duncan

Sharon Brown I REVIVAL SANCTUARY women embracing collaboration.
Founder at REVIVAL SANCTUARY for Women in Business | Editor in Chief at MO2VATE MAGAZINE | Founder at THE SPEAKERS INDEX | MD at LYDIAN EVENTS LTD | Best Selling Author | Member of BSME
March 14, 2021, Sharon Brown was a client of Winsome's

I have just had the pleasure of working with Winsome on our second book within Revival Sanctuary, namely, REVIVAL - Women Embracing Their Superpowers (Volume Two). From sign up to publishing, I found Winsome extremely efficient, knowledgeable and a pleasure to work with. As the date was nearing, I started to panic but Winsome reassured me and sure enough everything worked out perfectly. I would highly recommend using Winsome's publishing services as they are excellent value and this lady certainly knows her stuff. I'm looking forward to some collaborative work in the near future.

Selecting Your Marketing Campaign

Traditional publishers can take anywhere from 12 to 18 months to promote and market a book that is not fully written yet. Renowned British children's author Malorie Blackman recently signed to Merky Books Publishing in 2019 and announced her autobiography would be coming out in 2022. That is three years in waiting.

Stormzy's PRH imprint #Merky Books has snapped up Malorie Blackman's long-awaited autobiography.

William Heineman/#Merky Books editorial director Tom Avery acquired world rights for the as-yet untitled autobiography. The deal was negotiated by Hilary Delamere at The Agency (London) Ltd. Publication is slated for 2022.

One of Britain's best loved writers, for more than 30 years Blackman's books have helped shape British culture. She has sold 1.95 million books for £11.67m, with the 2006 paperback of *Noughts and Crosses* her bestseller at 299,644 copies sold.

Source: https://www.thebookseller.com/news/malorie-blackman-autobiography-goes-merky-books-1098821

When it comes to your marketing campaign the longer the better. However self-published authors always tend to be in a rush and are falling over themselves to get their book out. I know they are excited but there is a process to everything.

Express Marketing Campaign: For authors who are in a hurry to start earning money from their book and are too excited to wait.

Micro Marketing Campaign: For authors who want to make sure that they have enough time to organise and plan their launch and publicity.

Standard Marketing Campaign: For authors who understand the process of marketing lead times and are willing to give their books the best opportunity to shine.

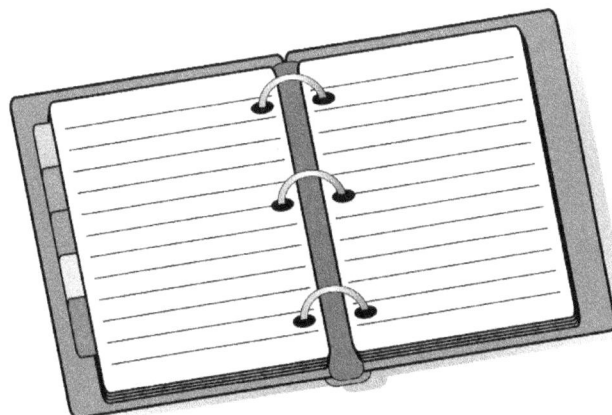

4 Weeks

Express

Campaign

Just Market It

Aim:

Objective:

Day Allocation	Time Allocation			
	AM	PM		Evening
Monday				
Tuesday				
Wednesday				
Thursday				
Friday				

Just Market It

Weekly Marketing Planner Week......			
Aim:			
Objective:			
Day Allocation	Time Allocation		
	AM	PM	Evening
Monday			
Tuesday			
Wednesday			
Thursday			
Friday			

Just Market It

Weekly Marketing Planner Week......			
Aim:			
Objective:			

Day Allocation	Time Allocation		
	AM	PM	Evening
Monday			
Tuesday			
Wednesday			
Thursday			
Friday			

Just Market It

Weekly Marketing Planner Week……			
Aim:			
Objective:			

Day Allocation	Time Allocation		
	AM	PM	Evening
Monday			
Tuesday			
Wednesday			
Thursday			
Friday			

8 Weeks

Micro

Campaign

Just Market It

Aim:

Objective:

Day Allocation	Time Allocation AM	PM	Evening
Monday			
Tuesday			
Wednesday			
Thursday			
Friday			

Just Market It

Weekly Marketing Planner Week......			
Aim:			
Objective:			
Day Allocation	**Time Allocation**		
	AM	PM	Evening
Monday			
Tuesday			
Wednesday			
Thursday			
Friday			

Just Market It

Weekly Marketing Planner Week......			
Aim:			
Objective:			

Day Allocation	Time Allocation		
	AM	PM	Evening
Monday			
Tuesday			
Wednesday			
Thursday			
Friday			

Just Market It

Aim:

Objective:

Day Allocation	Time Allocation			
	AM	PM		Evening
Monday				
Tuesday				
Wednesday				
Thursday				
Friday				

Just Market It

Weekly Marketing Planner Week......			
Aim:			
Objective:			

Day Allocation	Time Allocation		
	AM	PM	Evening
Monday			
Tuesday			
Wednesday			
Thursday			
Friday			

Just Market It

Aim:

Objective:

Day Allocation	Time Allocation			
	AM	PM		Evening
Monday				
Tuesday				
Wednesday				
Thursday				
Friday				

Just Market It

Weekly Marketing Planner Week......			
Aim:			
Objective:			
Day Allocation	Time Allocation		
	AM	PM	Evening
Monday			
Tuesday			
Wednesday			
Thursday			
Friday			

Just Market It

Weekly Marketing Planner Week......			
Aim:			
Objective:			
Day Allocation	Time Allocation		
	AM	PM	Evening
Monday			
Tuesday			
Wednesday			
Thursday			
Friday			

THE JUST
PUBLISH IT
FORMULA
BUSINESS
SET UP
TYPESETTING
TRAINING
GLOBAL BOOK
DISTRIBUTION
JUST
PUBLISH IT
Peaches
Publications
amazon.com
BEST
SELLING
BOOK
www.bookconfidencecoach.com

BECOME A
PUBLISHER
ONLINE COURSE
AUTHORS
EDITION
www.bookconfidencecoach.com

12 Weeks

Standard

Campaign

Just Market It

Weekly Marketing Planner Week......				
Aim:				
Objective:				

Day Allocation	Time Allocation			
	AM	PM		Evening
Monday				
Tuesday				
Wednesday				
Thursday				
Friday				

Just Market It

Weekly Marketing Planner Week......			
Aim:			
Objective:			

Day Allocation	Time Allocation		
	AM	PM	Evening
Monday			
Tuesday			
Wednesday			
Thursday			
Friday			

Just Market It

Weekly Marketing Planner Week……			
Aim:			
Objective:			

Day Allocation	Time Allocation		
	AM	PM	Evening
Monday			
Tuesday			
Wednesday			
Thursday			
Friday			

Just Market It

Weekly Marketing Planner Week......			
Aim:			
Objective:			

Day Allocation	Time Allocation		
	AM	PM	Evening
Monday			
Tuesday			
Wednesday			
Thursday			
Friday			

Just Market It

Weekly Marketing Planner Week……			
Aim:			
Objective:			

Day Allocation	Time Allocation		
	AM	PM	Evening
Monday			
Tuesday			
Wednesday			
Thursday			
Friday			

Just Market It

Weekly Marketing Planner Week......			
Aim:			
Objective:			

Day Allocation	Time Allocation		
	AM	PM	Evening
Monday			
Tuesday			
Wednesday			
Thursday			
Friday			

Just Market It

Weekly Marketing Planner Week......			
Aim:			
Objective:			

Day Allocation	Time Allocation		
	AM	PM	Evening
Monday			
Tuesday			
Wednesday			
Thursday			
Friday			

Just Market It

Weekly Marketing Planner Week......			
Aim:			
Objective:			
Day Allocation	Time Allocation		
	AM	PM	Evening
Monday			
Tuesday			
Wednesday			
Thursday			
Friday			

Just Market It

Aim:

Objective:

Day Allocation	Time Allocation			Evening
	AM	PM		
Monday				
Tuesday				
Wednesday				
Thursday				
Friday				

Just Market It

Weekly Marketing Planner Week......			
Aim:			
Objective:			
Day Allocation	**Time Allocation**		
	AM	PM	Evening
Monday			
Tuesday			
Wednesday			
Thursday			
Friday			

Just Market It

Weekly Marketing Planner Week……			
Aim:			
Objective:			

Day Allocation	Time Allocation		
	AM	PM	Evening
Monday			
Tuesday			
Wednesday			
Thursday			
Friday			

Just Market It

Weekly Marketing Planner Week......				
Aim:				
Objective:				
Day Allocation	**Time Allocation**			
	AM	PM		Evening
Monday				
Tuesday				
Wednesday				
Thursday				
Friday				

Become obsessed and be about that marketing life

Winsome Duncan

THE ROLLS ROYCE OF MARKETING

Always Be Closing (ABC)

People buy into you. Think about it – what motivated you to buy this book?

- ✓ Do you know of my work?
- ✓ Was it an advert online?
- ✓ Are you in my tribe?
- ✓ Was it a recommendation?
- ✓ Do you know me personally?
- ✓ Did Amazon recommend it to you?
- ✓ Was it a gift?

Whatever way this book got into your hands, remember that it serves a purpose you are looking for. It responds to a need or a pain that you have to advance your book career. Here are some of the reasons you might have brought this book:

- ✓ Raising your media profile.
- ✓ You are tired of not making sales.
- ✓ You are new to the book industry.
- ✓ You have yet to recoup your publishing investment.
- ✓ Maybe your sales have slowed down or stopped.

Anyhow, it is just you and I here because I have used the principle in my business to 'always be closing' (ABC). It is a great rule to know and get familiar with. As an author and businessperson, you must always have the end in mind. Steer the direction of the conversation so you can convert it to a sale. Stay focused. When you believe in your product and have done your absolute best, be steadfast and know that people out there want to buy what you have. You need to have confidence in your book business and always offer value. If you are teaching free courses, remember to share the 'what' and not the 'how'. Your tribe needs to invest in you to understand the intricate processes of your hard-earned knowledge. Always keep it in the back of your mind to ALWAYS BE CLOSING!

Low – Medium – High Price Points

Lesson number one: always upsell to your medium- to high-priced products and services, this must become second nature. If you do not remember anything else in this book, remember this simple thing: books do not sell. Sorry to break your heart but there it is the newsflash is out. You might get lucky and sell millions of books, but it is very unlikely, to be honest and if you do well, then good on you. So, in the meantime, you need to be creative around the ways in which you sell to your market. In our training I teach my clients how to look at the ways in which they can make money through their book. Here are some suggestions on how to expand your product and services:

- Create an online course
- Create workshops
- Create seminars
- Create conferences
- Create a book club
- Create a podcast
- Teach others how to write
- Become a consultant in your expertise
- Create a mastermind group
- Create retreats
- Create pamper and spa days
- Write a trilogy book series with a minimum of three books
- Write for blogs and newspapers
- Sell your content online
- Create a template bundle
- Create a colouring book
- Create journals

The idea here is to create several income streams to sell your book other than just a single product of one book.

Just Market It

Please proceed to list five new products and services in each category that will help increase your income streams. Take time and focus on your five-year vision when completing this table.

Products

	Low Price Point £5 - £499	Medium Price Point £500 - £2,499	High Price Point £2,500 +
Year 1			
Year 2			
Year 3			
Year 4			
Year 5			

Services

	Low Price Point £5 - £499	Medium Price Point £500 - £2,499	High Price Point £2,500 +
Year 1			
Year 2			
Year 3			
Year 4			
Year 5			

50 Call to Action Phases

What does a 'call to action' mean?

A call to action is a response or action you want to elicit from a client, prospect, or reader once they have encountered your brand. This approach is often used in a sale funnel and creates a sense of urgency when speaking to your customer pain points. A call to action is also known as CTA in its abbreviated format.

Here are some reasons why CTA would be beneficial for you:

- Build your mailing list by getting followers to sign up to your email
- Get your fans to follow your social media accounts
- Purchasing your products
- Investing in your services

You may now go on to customise the following CTA phrases for your social media platforms, for example:

Click here to find out how we did it (The Big Reveal)

Click here to read our FAQ (A tell-all question-and-answer session)

Click here to get the lowdown (informal: we are spilling the beans)

1. Download today
2. Last chance
3. Limited supply
4. Hurry! Only a few left
5. For a short time only
6. Order now and receive a free gift
7. See it in action
8. Click here for your free sample chapter
9. Ticket alert
10. Offer ends tomorrow
11. Act now

12. For a limited time only
13. One-time offer
14. Expires soon
15. Urgent action required
16. Start your free trial now
17. Sign up for your free trial immediately
18. Your free trial is just a click away
19. Join now and get...
20. Sign up now
21. Try before you buy
22. I invite you to...
23. We would like to hear from you
24. Join us today
25. Click here to get free shipping
26. Money-Back Guarantee
27. Best value today only
28. Limited availability
29. A one-time offer
30. Sign up online at...
31. Learn more about us at...
32. Order now while there is still time
33. In a hurry? Call us now...
34. We are waiting for your call
35. For more details, call...
36. Request your FREE quote today
37. Give us a call to find out all the details
38. Expires at midnight tonight
39. Sign up now while you still can
40. Call us this week to schedule an appointment
41. Deadline approaching
42. Hurry! Offer ends soon
43. Immediate download here...
44. Reply today and get...
45. Try it for free

46. Reserve your spot now
47. It is especially important that you respond promptly
48. The offer expires very soon
49. Only a few tickets left
50. Download your free eBook now

Copywriting

Copywriting is the act or occupation of writing text for the purpose of advertising or other forms of marketing. The product, called copy or sales copy, is written content that aims to increase brand awareness and ultimately persuade a person or group to take a particular action. **Source:** https://en.wikipedia.org/wiki/Copywriting

The first rule to copywriting is to make it about the end-user experience. You must consider the prospect and bring them into the sentence you are writing about for them to feel like the piece of copy text is relatable to them, their experience, and their pain points. Copywriting can become technical as you usually must make sure that you are using keyword planner words that are popular and trending. You need to make sure that the search terms within your copy are frequently used search terms as this will help you with your search engine optimisation when linked to your website. You need to make your prospects feel emotionally connected to and invested in the story that you are telling. It is important to explain the benefits and features of the product that you are selling. My advice to you is to learn online about copywriting or pay somebody to write it for you as it needs to be accurate.

On the next page, I want you to write 150 words of copy text for a free chapter of your book as a special offer to your network. Then I want you to reduce this copy to 100 words in your second draft and refine your sales pitch. Once you have completed this exercise, I want you to create a loss leader, collect and trade email data for a free chapter on your website.

Copywriting Sales Pitch

First Draft – 150 Words

Copywriting Sales Pitch – Second Draft – 100 Words

A Compelling Call-to-Action Copy

You can hire a freelance copywriter to create a catchy copy for you, or you can be brave and watch a few YouTube videos and use the information in this book to give it a go. Make sure your copy is extremely persuasive and remember to also incentivise them in your CTA. You will now create your call to action to buy your book and then write one for your service. Use the suggestions below to assist you:

Remember to bring the customer into your copy by using 'you'. For example, **'You'** can see the benefits....

- An Imaginative leap is a great way to attract attention, for example: Can you imagine...
- State the benefits and features of your product or service
- Use action words like 'now' or 'today' to translate to a higher click rate
- Make sure you are using words that are emotive and speaks to their pains
- Decide if your content will be inclusive or exclusive to your prospect

Call-To-Action Copy

Book Copy

Service Copy

Prospects Require Attentive Listening

Attentive listening is key when it comes to closing the sale with a potential prospect. You must make sure that you are fully conscious, awake, alert and paying attention because you want to be able to figure out if this prospect is the right fit for you. Be fully present in your interaction.

You must answer fair objections as to why they might not purchase from you. Show them not just the features but the benefits of what your product or service can do; you must offer an imaginative leap and get them to think about going into the future where their dreams and hopes live. Help them to see and feel the benefits of what your book, your coaching, your courses can do. Whatever the products or services, your prospect must feel like this will change their lives and improve them in some way. It is about *their* experience, not yours and making sure you meet their buying needs.

Do not be so quick to want to speak first; pause and wait for the prospect to conclude before you respond and feedback to them and reiterate what it is you heard them say. Have a notepad next to you and make some notes. You must create synergy by building rapport that makes them feel comfortable. Prospects do not buy from people they do not feel comfortable with; they buy from people they believe in and who address them in a professional, polite manner. Attentive listening is key when you have a prospect's need is placed in front of you. You need to quickly establish and decide whether your products or services can assist them.

I said that it is crucial to repeat what you hear them say because this allows you to make the connectors in your brain in terms of how you can support them effectively. Attentive listening is not about you wanting to jump in and say what you have to say because it is more important than your prospect's view. It is more about getting to know what their needs are and understanding if you can help them or not. This is a great skill to practise because it means that you are being present and in the moment. You are actively listening; you are not thinking about what you will cook that evening for dinner. You are just focusing on their needs and how you can be of service to them. I use this technique a lot in my work because it helps me to network better. We have two ears and one mouth for a reason.

Just Market It

A Media Press Pack

A book media press pack consists of three things:

1. A press release
2. An Author Information sheet (AI)
3. 3D promotional book advert placements
4. Colour pictures
5. Black and white pictures
6. Short biography

Do you have a media press pack, yes or no?

Yes	No
Explain why?	Explain why?

If your answer is 'no', I am not really surprised at this point. My question to you is, *why* do you not have a press release as the bare minimum? Please explain this to me. If you do have a media press pack, what is the purpose of it?

These are just the basic things to be implemented into your book business to propel your book sales forward; it is not rocket science. However, it is a good way for you to engage with the press, build a relationship, and get the press responding back to you. Whenever you are putting together a media pack, it is always good to make sure you have an Author Information sheet (AI). This is different to a biography. If you want to be fancy, you can pay someone to design your pack so that it is nicely colour co-ordinated, matches with your brand colours and looks professional. Remember how I shared a small section of my press life with you, I did that with a compelling media press pack. If you are struggling with this pack, this service is available for you to purchase here:

http://www.peachespublications.co.uk/media-press-pack.html

Do you know whenever I am sending a press release out, I always think about all the content I need to include in this press release first? Then I think about who I am sending it to and how I can leverage the message that I am trying to get across. I suggest that you enrol in our online course so I can teach you how to create a media press pack that includes developing your core message and author brand story. I have left the link in the reference section for you to watch a YouTube video. This will help you see an example of how to construct an effective press release.

Remember, do not overload your press release; keep it to one A4 page. Have a clear message; the strapline should be catchy; three paragraphs beginning, middle and end and then have a call to action. Always put your contact details at the bottom. Add quotes from you or someone famous pertinent to the subject matter. Make sure you directly send it to a person as opposed to a generic email because people hardly ever look at generic emails. Above all, be persistent.

You will need to create a press list with a minimum of ten company names; more is ideal. Be sure to spellcheck your press release. Make sure you follow it up; do not feel you are harassing them. Remember, they get hundreds of emails. My number one secret is to email a journalist first thing in the morning so that you go straight to the top of the pile. You need to make an Excel spreadsheet of all your journalist contacts and follow up regularly.

Just Market It

Write down ten media outlets to approach this table:

Press list	Address	Telephone/ Email	Contact person
1.			
2.			
3.			
4.			
5.			
6.			
7.			
8.			
9.			
10.			

3D Book Placement Adverts

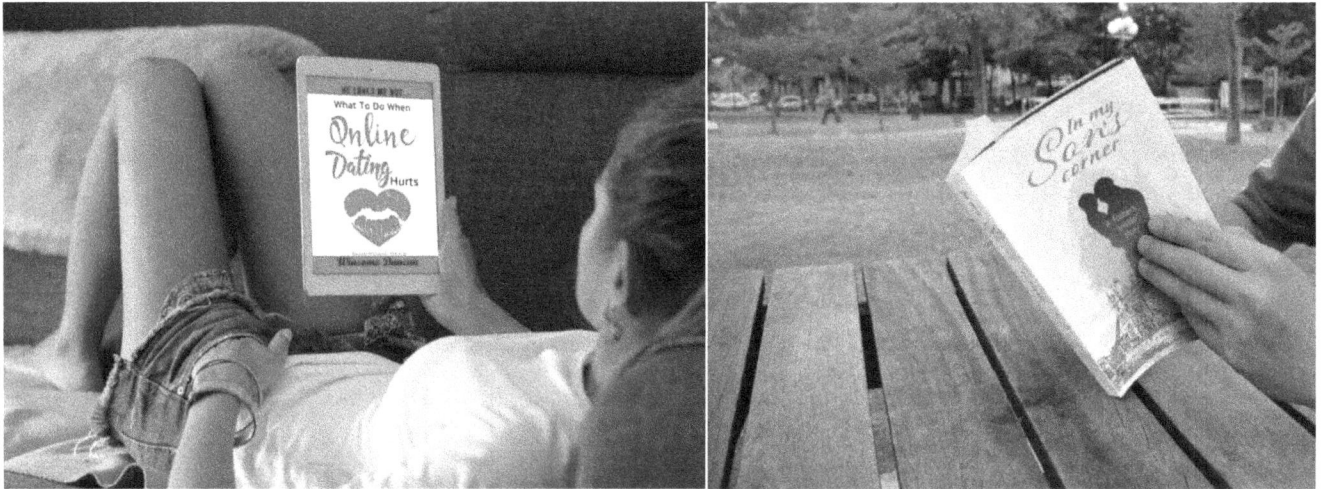

These are great for changing the look of the book online, and they make sure your supporters never get tired of seeing the same images. 3D images are better than flat book covers, and placement images make for an interesting view.

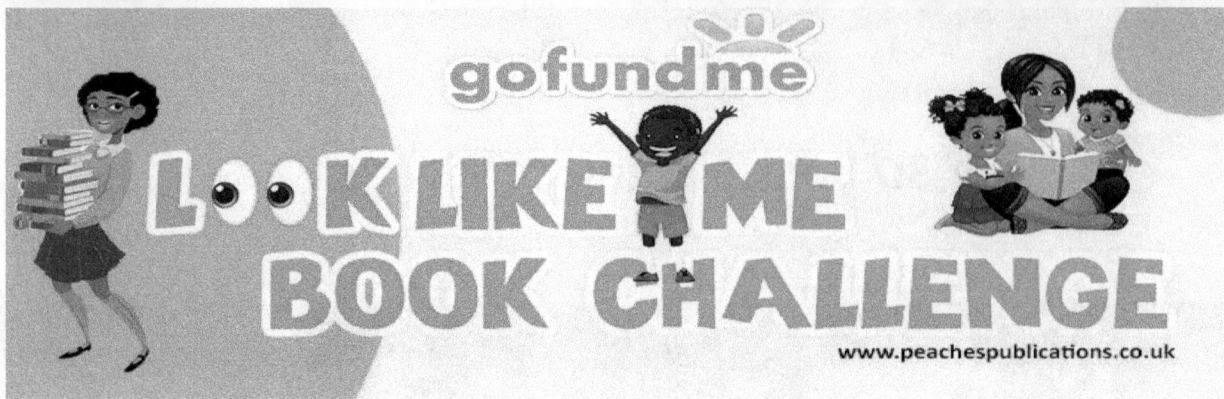

Sample Press Release

November 2019

Visual Representation for BAME Main Characters in Children's Storybooks is a MUST!

5% of BAME main characters are in children's books, compared to the 33.5% of BAME children that are in the UK educational school system. Guardian September 2019.

The research team at the Centre of Literacy in Primary Education writes the **Reflecting Realities Report** which highlighted this cataphoric marginalised percentage. We acknowledge this statistic is unacceptable, we are teaching our **BAME young people** that their stories are **irrelevant** by continually **underrepresenting** them in fairy tales, where their imagination lives.

Award-winning author Winsome Duncan has a passion to be a part of the solution by changing this dreadful statistic. She wants to gather 30 children ages **7-11 years old** to create one book through **play, storytelling, character building** and **artwork design**. The **Look Like Me Book Challenge** has been set up via **Go Fund Me** to raise **£10,000** to support **young authors** and to offer an opportunity for our mini-Entrepreneurs to earn extra pocket money through the sales of their books.

Our Look Like Me Manifesto is simple:

- To increase the diversity of main characters in children's books to 10% over the next three years
- To create a BAME author association to support UK authors
- To get corporate publishing houses/bookshops to offer a diverse book selection

Help us **raise awareness** by interviewing us, sharing our campaign, and making a **generous donation**: https://www.gofundme.com/f/look-like-me-book-challenge

Contact: CEO Winsome Duncan of Peaches Publications is available for interviews for television, radio, news features, panel discussions, newspaper, and magazines.

Website: www.looklikeme.co.uk

Telephone: XXXXXXX

Email: XXXXXXXXXXX

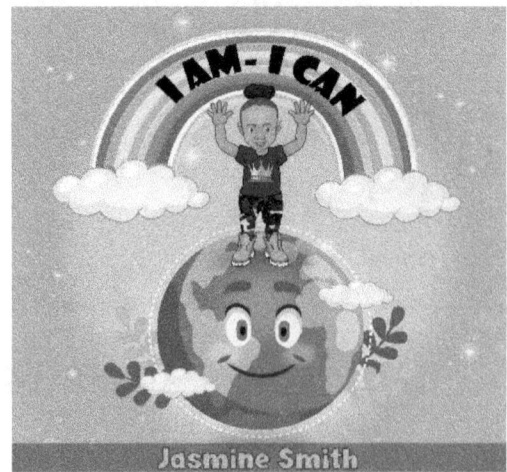

125

Just Market It

Press Release Template

PRESS RELEASE SHOULD BE NO MORE THAN AN A4 PAGE

PRESS RELEASE: - Always write this.

Date: - I like to start from the 1st of the month, you can choose daily.

Strapline: - Make it clear and concise.

Quotes: – If necessary, embed them in the body text.

Opening paragraph 1: – Who are you and what do you do?

Statistics: - 1 or 2 where necessary, always quote the source.

Middle Paragraph 2: – Tell us about your book and why we should care.

Concluding Paragraph 3: – Create a compelling conclusion.

CALL TO ACTION: Write your contact details and what media coverage you are available for.

This means the end of the press release and is placed in the middle.

###

Author Information (AI)

An Author Information (AI) sheet is used to pre-promote your book before its release. It is important to have an author picture so that you are easily identifiable. You need to include the proposed release date—you can be vague and say 'winter 2026' to give you more wiggle room for rewrites or errors. Be sure to mention who the publisher is.

Give the contacts that you have, some insight into when the book is coming out, so that they can schedule reviews, features or advertisements, and help you make sure you are not going in from a cold story angle. It is traditional to have an Author Information (AI) sheet alongside a press release.

A Biography and an Autor Information have two different objectives; please do not get confused when writing this out. Remember to include:

- Projected book launch
- A professional author picture
- Who the Publisher is
- A brief overview of what the book is about
- Contact details
- Offer an excerpt

"If you sell to everyone, you sell to no one."

Meredith Hill

Branding with Lily

So, what has branding got to do with being an author?

Everything!

And here is what you need to know…

If branding is the spiritual home for all marketing, public relations, and advertising efforts, then our logo, website, flyers, social media and how we present ourselves are the signposts that lead to the holy grail of engagement with our target audience and prospects. It is a no-brainer that you must check our brands first before anything else.

I would say that, right. Because all I do is talk and teach about branding, both personal and for business. As an author, you become the AUTHORity of your chosen subject matter. This is more so for non-fiction books. In this case, I will refer to branding for you and for your book or books as the case may be and how you could navigate its spiritual journey. Besides, there will be a mini case study for a brand-new author with recommendations just for you. Let us get started.

If you have come this far to finish your book, you might be forgiven in thinking that the journey is complete, and your job is done. Wrong! In fact, the opposite is true. If you want your book to do well, great branding should have been developed in tandem with the writing and publishing process. It will ensure that you will, by default, be the flag-bearer of the content and ultimately speak on behalf of the book and all that it stands for.

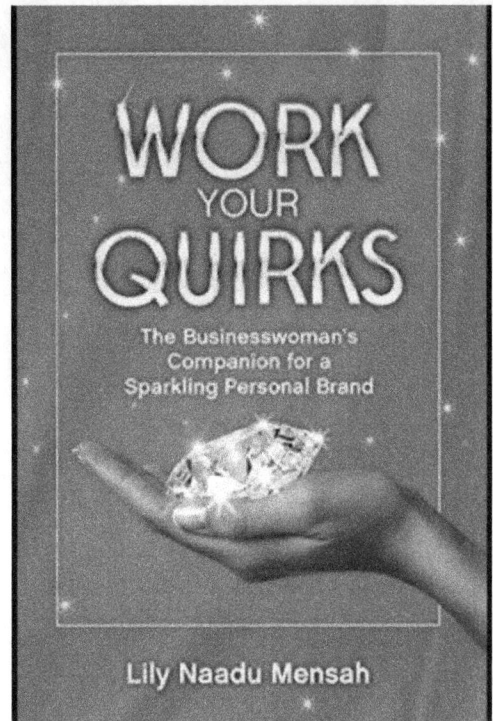

To be known for something, you must stand out from the crowd. How do you do that when numerous others purport to do the same thing? You may be the only one doing what you are doing right now, but in no time, especially if you are successful, someone somewhere will copy or try to emulate what you have worked your butt off to create, which is not fair. Fear not. If you get your branding on point, they can copy as much as they like, but they will never be you because you have the copyright of **Brand YOU**. Let us delve deeper into what is in my mind, what an A.U.T.H.O.R. acronym stands for and how to build and engage with others, so your brand shows up with pizazz and stardust.

A: AUTHORity – We have all grown up and been taught to look up to authority figures in our lives. Some of us have rebelled against them at times; however, one thing for sure is that we do not forget them. They make us think, and we make decisions either to be one of their followers or ex-followers. They challenge our thinking and always give us food for thought. They can never be all things to all men, women, and children. It is time to bring into the fray your specialist knowledge as to why you should be seen as the authority expert in your chosen field. Accolades within your sector are a positive reflection for your peers to witness.

U: Ubiquitous – This translates to you being the go-to person for your subject matter. The all hail, reigning King or Queen of your brand. It demonstrates brand excellence. You must own that space and work it like your life depends on it. Your logo, your book cover, your communication should scream, **I know my stuff inside out, and you call me if you need further information about my book or how to access my services.** You tell it like it is, straight, no chaser, and take no prisoners and above all, be authentically YOU. You always bring colour and life to your brand. You tell it to everyone who will listen. You draw a crowd around you like bees to honey. You enlist the help of your brand evangelists – those who will endorse and recommend you, this is key. You need to be on your audience radar long before you finish the book, so they are ready to help you start the promotion process and of course when it hits the book stands. Your brand evangelists will be your foot soldiers and help carry your message to the masses.

T: Teacher – In getting your book published, you may be seen as a teacher of your subject because you are already slaying it, right? Well, if you do not go out and promote your book and say yes to every opportunity presented, everything you ever thought about marketing has not been disrupted. Good teachers inspire others to do what they dream of or attempt what they never even thought of. What sort of message are you sending out? Is it inspiring? Are you able to recite text from your book if you were ambushed in an underground car park as your get-out clause? Having a catchphrase that automatically links the book to you. Do you know what will that be?

H: Humanity – Why do we read books? And why would I pick your book up instead of the other from the proverbial bookshelf? There is often a human element as to who wrote the book and why? What is your why, and how are you selling that why? It is the connection between your words and your reader. Get the connection right, and you are likely to appeal to your target audience; that is, assuming you have done some groundwork around that subject previously in the JUST WRITE IT workbook. People buy people, and as much as your publishing house might do all the PR, etc. for you, you will still have to show up for the book signing. They cannot do it for you, so your humanity is so important in getting the books off the shelf and into your readers' hands.

O: Ownership – In asserting your rights as the owner of the material, you are telling the world that you are, in fact, in charge of this, and the buck stops with you. As a Brand, it is vital that you make this part of the everyday language. You become an orator who tells the story around the content. This can be in speaking engagements, your literature, your email signature, website, and you should start to say, "I am an authority on this subject, and my book is... and this is where you can grab a copy."

R: Relevant – You might want to skip through various stages of capturing your target audience's imagination, and try as you might, it is easy to forget that if it is not relevant to them at a particular time of day, it will not move them to imbibe your well-crafted words. Words you would no doubt have agonised over and edited to within an inch of your life. Words carry power. Ask yourself, how relevant is the message that you are telling your potential buyers? Do people need to hear your stuff, and if they do, how will it change their thinking, and will they take action to make a purchase?

Why don't we have a look at a case study of an author who is just about to publish her book and how she can stand out as an AUTHORrity in her market!

Case study: Mellie K. aka The Food Stylist – Author of The Healthy Caribbean Cookbook

Mellie K. is about to launch her book on healthy African-Caribbean Cuisine. How does she brand herself for the pre-launch and post-launch to ensure her book is successful? A brief summary of what she might consider as an AUTHORity:

AUTHORity: She is passionate about healthy food choices without compromising on century-old staples and is armed with a degree in biological sciences. We all respect scientists, and my recommendation is to amplify her scientific prowess in her brand strategy. A food stylist is good; however, I would aim for something sassier.
'Soul-food Scientist' might be another option? There is an alliteration there too.

Ubiquitous: She will have to show up in all the areas, and to the people she needs to convince that she is the authority. This involves her previous clients, friends, colleagues, suppliers, foodies, ambassadors, and brand evangelists. A strong online presence is absolutely a must, and it should be prolific leading up to the launch and beyond. If you feel uncertain, outsource your social media, and gain full traction.

<u>Teacher:</u> Quick tease videos, photos and sample recipes will excite and promote the brand. This should also help with recall from book buyers. The book will eventually become her calling card which she should carry everywhere with her as proof, especially in the first year of publishing. That will be like the AMEX card advert. Do not leave home without your book; it must be glued to you at all times publicly.

<u>Humanity:</u> We all buy people, and I would like to know the person behind the brand and what is her why. As a health and wellbeing specialist, Mellie K. should let her audience know her raison d'être. In this case, it is to reach more people who are obese or who suffer from diabetes and other illnesses with her message of healthy food without compromise.

<u>Ownership:</u> To own the brand, Mellie K. must own the overall message. Naming, logo, book cover, etc., should reflect the content. African-Caribbean food is very colourful and full of spices. I'd think of adding words like 'flavour', 'sauce', 'soul food and the like to the content by telling the story of food, family, fun and friendship. I would recommend a cover that shows food placement or eating together.

<u>Relevant:</u> Many of us want to keep fit and healthy, yet have our chicken, rice, and peas, ackee and plantain. We will need to be convinced not to fry everything yet still smell and taste the goodness. 'Sell the sizzle, not the sausage', as they say—this will never be truer in this regard. This could translate into 'you can have

it all, but just a 'little bit healthier'. I would certainly spend my money on that promise alone.

When all is said and done, I want to congratulate you all on coming this far; many have their books in their heads, on laptops, on paper or even in notebooks. You have taken the leap of faith in yourself and penned it and published it. Whoop-whoop and congratulations!

Remember to quote 'QUIRKY' when you reach out to me.

Good luck,

Lily Naadu Mensah

HONEY IN YOUR MONEY

Book Inventory

Besides Amazon's Sales Reports that you can print out, how will you manage your book inventory? I am asking you this because it is important to know how many books you are selling at any given time. It is a good business practice to stay on top of your records, regarding your income and expenditure.

I do my book inventory through excel spreadsheets; my mentor taught me how to do this, and it has been an extremely useful tool for me. I have used it over the years to submit budgets and keep an inventory of books sold. Any good business, as standard practice, will keep detailed records of sales. Books are no different, and if you are upselling your products – for example, courses, hardback books, paperback books, mugs, cards and so forth – make sure you have a breakdown of costs for each product, how much you are selling them for and what the profit margin on each product is.

When you sell a book direct to your customer for £10, and you paid £3.50 for manufacture costs and delivery, your profit margin would be £6.50. However, if you had to pay additional postage and packaging of £1.50, which included your envelope and stamps, your profit margin would be £5. Getting to grips with your figures and making sure you understand how to capture your data helps you and helps HMRC Taxman. Check out Lisa Newton from Boogles Accounting for all your accounting and bookkeeping needs: www.boogles.co.uk.

Card Readers

Move with the times. Contactless card readers are the way to go now. If you are old school like I was, I used a phone app because PayPal card readers are expensive. However, I wanted PayPal Service App because I do not want to have to sit and wait three working days for my money to be transferred into my account. I need instant access to my funds.

There are some ways that you can get around reducing the cost.

I love me some PayPal it is my best friend. In days of old, I downloaded the PayPal HERE app and manually put in the buyer's card details; however, this was quite time-consuming. I felt funny holding people's cards in a contactless age, and more importantly, if I made a mistake, I had to start again.

I desperately wanted to buy a PayPal contactless reader for a long time; however, I stayed with the mindset of 'if it is not broke, do not try to fix it'. You may remember that when their first card reader came out, you could swipe and then tap your pin, well mine did not work, and it kept losing its charge and having no reception. So, I was not a fan of this product and never got back the £79.99 that I spent.

What I did was I went on to eBay, and I purchased a second-hand reader for £26. It was listed as brand new, never been used before. I was incredibly happy with this offer. Yes, there are other readers out there like Square, and I think that they are £29.99; however, they do not put the money in your bank straight away. This is why I love me some PayPal because PayPal knows what time it is, and as soon as you get paid, you can transfer the money into your account straight away unless it is a e-cheque. There are no delays on this, so think about the convenience.

The moral of the story is you need to purchase a contactless card reader and invest properly in your book business, just like you have purchased this workbook. Remember stalls will be opening soon and we will have that one-to-one contact.

Websites

I am not a website expert so let us get that out the way. However, I know how to do basic HTML coding and drop-and-drag template designs. I understand the importance and value of having a website, and I understand the problem of having a low budget. When I first started my business, Peaches Publications, I used a free E-Commerce website, and I was able to sell via it for the first two years as I was still testing my services and was not sure if I wanted to spend extra money on yet another website.

My free website looked like this www.weebley.peachespublications.com, and it served its purpose for that time. If you are struggling, you can consider these options. Eventually, I decided to take my business seriously after two years as I could see the growth potential. A good quality website can cost you thousands of pounds, and it is good to have an opt-in website which simply means you can capture prospects' data. Once you have an email address, you can place your prospects into your sales funnel for higher conversion rates.

Landing Page

A landing page is not a website, please do not confuse the two. The purpose of a landing page is to sell a product or service with one objective and a single call to action. They are typically used to sign up for courses or to purchase discounted products. They are great for loss leaders as well; providing a freebie and capturing email data is so valuable. Your first target should be 1000 sign-ups to your mailing list.

Income Streams

Multiple income streams are an interesting subject for me. I find it fascinating how you can generate mass revenue from one tiny book that you have written. I am going to show you the ways in which I have been successful at earning thousands of pounds. The list below has everything I did to increase my book wealth. During this process, I want you to go away and think carefully about how you can generate your own three extra income streams. Using the 5 key points on the next page, be sure to plot your process. Write down your top three income generators. You can use items on this list or other ideas you may have:

1. Create workshops on platforms using Zoom or Microsoft Teams
2. Create online seminars
3. Create online conferences
4. Create online summits
5. Create online VIP coaching sessions
6. Create online mastermind groups
7. Create half-day and full-day masterclasses
8. Write a book series of 3 - 7 book minimum
9. Partnership with the Mayor's Office
10. Sell publishing packages
11. Create online courses
12. Paid speaking engagements
13. Perform your poetry or song
14. Become a Consultant
15. Become a Coach

Now it is your turn to take the time out to create your own list of ways to go ahead and upscale your income streams based on the knowledge, expertise, and confidence that you have been taught from your book. For example, even if it is a fiction, you can teach another person how to write fiction, and that could be your upsell and area of expertise.

Just Market It

Income Generator 1	Income Generator 2	Income Generator 3

5 Key Points	5 Key Points	5 Key Points

The World Is Your Stage

You must understand that the world is waiting to hear your message. The fact that you can go onto YouTube and reach an international audience with one video is amazing. It is like having your own television station at your fingertips. You must use your voice to go out into the world and spread the message God has placed inside of your heart. You have one voice, one vibration, so go ahead and use it. Be the voice to the voiceless and be determined to tell your story to anyone who will listen with an unwavering passion. Transport yourself out of your comfort zone; stop sitting on the side-lines; own your space and soar. Voice projection takes time to master; it is a skill that is well worth it. Here are some tips to consider when speaking on stage or on Zoom to your audience:

1. Sit or stand up straight.
2. Do not use filler words in between sentences like 'um' and 'er'. It sounds unprofessional and shows your nerves.
3. Speak at a volume just above your normal speaking voice.
4. Prepare your presentation a few nights in advance.
5. Connect with your audience by sharing emotive stories.
6. Get some training from top professional speakers like I did.
7. Have an engaging voice that changes pitch.
8. Use the texture and dexterity of your voice to pull listeners into the story.
9. Talk about your personal story.
10. Remember, humour goes a long way, do implement laughter.
11. Act confident even if you are not.
12. Look your listeners in the eye, even on screen.
13. Smile with your eyes.
14. Speak from the heart.
15. Invest in a ring light so you can have the correct lighting.

Public Presentation Skills

I have taken the time to invest in myself and learn the art of public speaking, which has been extremely beneficial to me. I have been able to use my charm, charisma, and wit to open many doors. Although I sometimes feel nervous, this is natural no matter how many times you go on stage and speak. Luckily for me, I have trained with motivational speaker and legend Mr Les Brown, who has amassed a $65,000,000 fortune from speaking. I also trained with the great Andy Harrington at Speaker's Academy. I learnt some phenomenal tips on how to dominate stage left and stage right. These investments are key to raising your profile as an author.

Accountability Partner

If you are serious about achieving your book marketing goals and making sure that you are working on your campaign every week, it is important to get an accountability partner to work with you. They must be a success in business or a prolific author. Better still, you can hire a mentor if you have the budget. You need to talk once a week or biweekly and make sure you are ticking off your plan. A good accountability partner will not allow you to slack off. Keep your calls between 30 to 60 minutes, stay focused and stick to the things-to-do list. What makes a good accountability partner?

- Commitment
- Communication
- Ideas generator
- Focus
- A proactive writer
- A person who enjoys research
- Dedication
- Hardworking
- Gives constructive criticism
- Encouraging
- An attentive listener

Book Embellishment

I love the word 'embellishment'; it can change the whole trajectory of a book in a short space of time. I always see embellishment as decoration or the cherry on top of the cake. It helps to give your book definition, texture, and dexterity. It paints a pretty picture if done correctly. Now it is time to transfer those skills over into your copywriting, advertising, and marketing of your book. This is crucial when describing your book on social media and making it sound interesting.

Let me give you a mobile text example:

Hi there, I would like you to come to my book launch on Saturday 27th 2020 at 7.00 p.m.; please can you respond below if you can attend? Thank you.

I am sure you would agree that sounds a little dry. Here is the embellishment example:

Hi Kemi, I hope all is well in your world. I am super excited to tell you that my debut book launch is on Saturday 27th March at 7.00 p.m. Tickets are free and available on Eventbrite. I have written a book about helping you to realign with your purpose, and it is called The Awakening. There will be an opportunity to network at this event which will be full of inspiration. Can I count on you to attend?

Can you see that there is much more flavour and engagement here because it paints a clearer picture? Please write down the key elements that were added in the second text below:

1	2	3	4	5

Templates Are Your Best Friend

Sometimes in life, you have just got to take the easy road. By that, I mean try to find a quick and convenient way to do the things you need to do that otherwise would cost a lot of money. I love using Canva—there I said it. Canva is simply amazing; you can use the free version or get the professional version, depending on your needs. Canva has changed my life, and I love it.

This website has thousands of templates for you to choose a suitable design, banners, flyers, posters, wedding invitations and moving animation videos, journals, and so much more. You simply type in what kind of event you want—let us say, for example, a book launch, and it will display all the book launch templates that you can use, you just need to replace the text and the images. They even have low-cost stock images you can purchase and use for yourself, copyright free.

I use Canva to create flyers that I need in a hurry. If I have a television or radio appearance coming up, I create the flyers using this site. If I am doing a seminar, workshop, or conference I create the flyers on Canva for individual speakers as it can be quite costly to get a designer to do them all. Normally I would pay the designer to do the main flyer and then circulate it. Do not be afraid to test the outcome; sit down for a couple of hours, watch some video tutorials, play around with the templates and colour schemes, experiment with the gradient and create some inspiring images with their wonderful designs. My brand story image was made on Canva and my Marketer Avatar text on the right was the same.

If you are a confused Marketer Avatar and feel overwhelmed, it is time to get over your fear or you can outsource the job to Upwork or Fiverr; however, there is a cost that you will need to pay. I have placed the link at the back of the book in the reference section. Good luck and enjoy.

Bulk Buy Book Sales

As an author, think big! Make the mindset of one, two or three book sales redundant. I want you to think about bulk buy book sales going forward in your marketing journey. Yes, on Amazon, it is great to have those sales coming in; it all adds up to your royalties at the end of the month. Let Amazon put effort into sending out your books in small amounts and posting them to your customers. You need to find a way to contact book clubs or book wholesalers that specialise in selecting books each month for their audiences. To buy in bulk from a printer significantly reduces the unit price per book. You will never get rich sending one or two books here and there or selling a few at festivals; you really have to draw down into your niche market.

I want you to make a list of ten book wholesalers that you can approach to see if they are willing to purchase copies of your book in advance. You can go onto Instagram or Google and just type in 'book wholesalers' and 'book distributors'. You will be required to give a discount on your recommended retail price of anywhere between 55% and 30% depending on where you go. The bigger the author connection is, the more money they would want to discount to their audience. When we brought the book *The Popcorn House,* we bought and invested in 1,000 copies simply because we had 30 young children and their parents involved in this project; this brought the cost of the unit price down to a more affordable price for families, and we could meet the standards of most wholesalers' prices which are anywhere from £1.00 to £3.50 per copy of the book.

Be sure to follow up with an email if you have not heard from them in a week and again in another two weeks, and if they have not got back to you by then, then revisit them in a month or give them a call to remind them. You must be persistent, do not think you are bugging them or making a nuisance of yourself; this is business, and they have the funds to support this. This is a prime time to be selling your book because people are at home and have time to read or they are off work and are furloughed. You need to be taking advantage of this and allow your business to expand with bigger volumes.

Sale on Return (SOR)

SOR is an abbreviation for 'sale on return'. Authors feel different ways about this; for me personally, it does not work. I remember having my book in a few shops across the UK and just never collecting the money, never invoicing the owners, and I just did not have the time to chase. It was just one or two units, maybe three, so whenever I provide books to stores, I request they buy them advanced stock and not do sale on return. At the end of each month, nobody wants to take the time out to contact all the bookstores and ask repeatedly, have you sold my book? Invoicing can be quite tiresome. My advice is that you find a bookseller that sells books in your category/genre, be it children's books or adult fiction for Black authors, and you get them to make a bulk order for which they will pay you in advance. A minimum of twenty sales in advance is worthwhile. This will help you avoid the back and forth for small numbers like three or four books. You want to get bulk sales moving forward. 100 units sold is my largest bulk book buy to date.

Outsourcing

You can outsource your marketing to freelancers and get them to assist you in building your brand by, creating flyers, creating banners, producing free eBooks, and so much more. You must understand the limits of your skillset. In your book business, you need to know how everything works, but you do not have to do it all yourself. You must build a reliable team around you to create and implement an effective marketing campaign. When you are outsourcing online, it can sometimes be hit or miss, and you really must have a vision of what you are trying to create with your tribe. The best advice I can give you, is to think solution based, always look at the ways in which you can solve a problem. There is an answer to most problems let us say challenges instead. If you open your 'I Can' mindset up to them, you will be able to progress quickly on your business journey.

Just Market It

Wholesalers List

Company Name	Date	Outcome

"If you can look up you can get up".

Les Brown

Handling Rejection Like a Boss

"Every no brings you closer to a yes." – Mark Cuban

NO Formula: N+O = New Opportunity

From my years of experience, I can say, hand on heart, try not to take it personally if someone does not believe in your book vision. You do not need anyone else to co-sign your dreams. Journalists are overwhelmingly busy with daily emails, phone calls, and deadlines. Remember, your book is not for everyone; it is written for a select audience, and once you understand that audience, you can go out into the world and achieve so many great things.

As an empath and a hypersensitive person, I frequently struggle with rejection, and I have had to learn that what is for me cannot be taken away. I now use and transform the word 'no' as a 'new opportunity' to get closer to my objectives and goals around the publishing industry with the promotions of my books. If someone's feedback is: 'There were grammar or spelling errors' or 'I did not like the graphics in the book', then listen to them; they are your buyers. It may mean that you need to do a complete rewrite, and it is fine to have a second edition of your book if you believe it will sell. Practice change till you get it right.

We have two ears and one mouth for a reason, and the sooner you can learn attentive listening to support your clients', your customers', and your buyers' needs, the more successful you will be. How can you be disheartened at the first hurdle of your book marketing journey? Come on! Buck up your ideas.

The traditional publishers sometimes market books in advance for anywhere between one year to eighteen months whilst the book is being written. A self-published author's marketing campaign or pre-launch can be anywhere from one month to three months. I would suggest trying to go somewhere in the middle, like six weeks, due to author excitement. However, if you are still writing a book, you can have a longer lead time of three months or more, and this is the boss approach because you are methodical in your process. Pre-sales are a great way to gain attention for you pending title and earn advance income.

I remember being rejected by several traditional publishers with my first book, *123 Back to Me,* which was about self-healing, and it remains unpublished yet. I still have the rejection letters, which put me on the path of writing my own books and becoming a self-published author and eventually turning into a hybrid publisher. You never know where the next 'no' will take you! Embrace the process and have a positive mental attitude. Be encouraged, and you may need to tweak your reader avatar some more to make sure you are in the right target market.

Paid Advertising on Social Media

To advertise correctly was a huge learning curve even for me. You can advertise with an advert on a YouTube video or with a YouTube textbox advert. You can advertise as a sponsored story on Instagram, and you can advertise your own direct post on Instagram with a campaign outcome to attract more likes and followers. Then there is the grand old Facebook which filters your messages to only 10% of your friendship group, making you feel like no one is engaging in your posts. Then it suggests making it easy for you to advertise by them selecting your core audience based on your algorithms. Whichever way it swings, you are going to- have to invest in your book business. You are going to need to know how you are going to reach your target market.

Facebook is great for getting more eyes on your work when you spend thousands of pounds with them, and you would need to hire an ad team to help you learn the specifics of algorithms and demographics. This is where it gets super technical. We are not going to dive into the advanced stages of advertising; however, I believe your best option is to simply learn how to advertise your book on Amazon as they have millions of buyers waiting to buy what you have.

Google ads have vouchers for £75 off if you spend £25.00 with them. In total, this is £100 worth of advertising, but you have got to know the target audience you want to reach. When you download the app, you can see the pre-setup advertising tool where you select your demographic, location, age, etc. yourself. Be mindful to select correctly; they have an advanced Google ad for professionals; this is where you hire someone to manage your account. I went in blindly before. I spent the £100 and the only call back I got was from a wrong number; no one contacted me via my website. It was so disappointing. I long to get the word out far and wide about what I do, yet I just keep missing the mark with paid advertisements. I feel strongly about training and learning what you do not know or paying a professional to move you up in the SEO (Search Engine Optimisation) ranking.

There is no getting around it; you need to spend hundreds – if not thousands – of pounds on advertising; that is how the big boys get their books out there into the public domain and monetise with the upsell from the small-price product. They are making six figures, and it is as simple as that. You also need to understand in-depth who your ideal customer avatar is.

As said earlier in one of the quotes, if you sell to anyone, you sell to no one because 'anyone' is not your target audience. You must be specific and clear on how you are going to reach out to them. My suggestion at this stage as a beginner moving into intermediate is to not really mess around with Facebook, Instagram, or YouTube. Go and learn how to advertise in the American Amazon marketplace and then in the UK Amazon marketplace. Amazon marketing tools have a friendly interface; you just need to learn about negative and positive keywords and remember to google what you do not know. That is how I have accumulated my knowledge: by online training. Below is what the Amazon interface looks like.

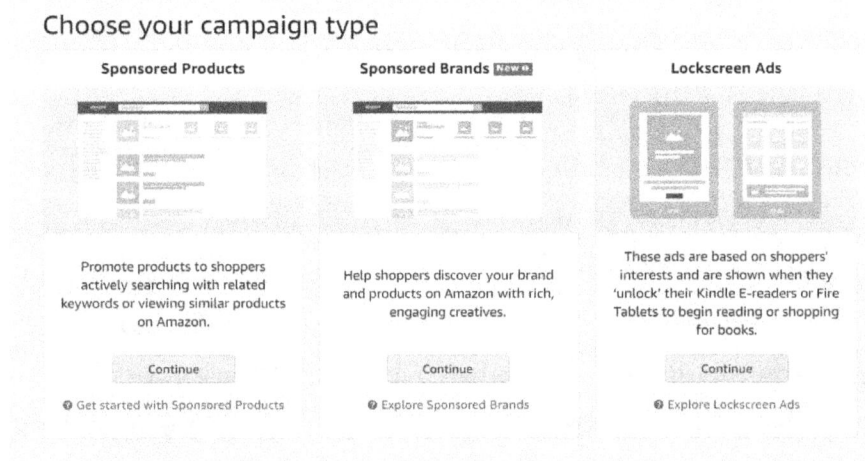

Choose your campaign type

Sponsored Products — Promote products to shoppers actively searching with related keywords or viewing similar products on Amazon. Continue — Get started with Sponsored Products

Sponsored Brands New — Help shoppers discover your brand and products on Amazon with rich, engaging creatives. Continue — Explore Sponsored Brands

Lockscreen Ads — These ads are based on shoppers' interests and are shown when they 'unlock' their Kindle E-readers or Fire Tablets to begin reading or shopping for books. Continue — Explore Lockscreen Ads

Website as at June 2021

Everyone is not your target audience; this is an amateur mistake. Our advance JUST MARKET IT online course will go into this subject more because it remains specialist. You can sign up here:

www.bookconfidencecoach.com

"Your
network
is your net worth."

Tim Sanders

Increase Your Sales 4 Weeks Challenge

It is time to get proactive and increase your sales in our 30-day challenge.

- Are you up for the challenge?
- Are you up for the tasks?
- Are you ready to go to the next level with your book?

By now, you should have a great deal of information to begin to implement and start to see changes within your income streams. I guess the question now becomes do you want to do what it takes to diversify and earn more money? Remember your commitment gauge at the beginning of the book? What does that number look like now, knowing that only 40% of you will rise to the challenge?

I am going to give you a challenge. For the next 30 days, I would like you to think of new and inventive ways to increase your income by at least a minimum of 10% this month. Using the chart below, I want you to track your daily sales for one month. You can begin to monetise your income streams using: a loss leader, free eBook, free audio download, follow up warm or hot leads, you decide.

Log your sales figures on the daily sales table on the next page.

Just Market It

Daily Sales Table

1	2	3	4	5	6	**7**	**Week 1 Total £**
8	9	10	11	12	13	14	**Week 2 Total £**
15	16	17	18	19	20	21	**Week 3 Total £**
22	23	24	25	26	27	28	**Week 4 Total £**

Just Dominate

As we reach the end of our time together, you and your book must be set apart. What I mean by this is that you need to stand out from the rest of the crowd of authors with excellent cover designs and brand appeal. Readers should be falling over themselves to give you their hard-earned money. Be nothing less than a force of nature, and if you do not know how, you need to quickly learn. Let us look at the word dominate.

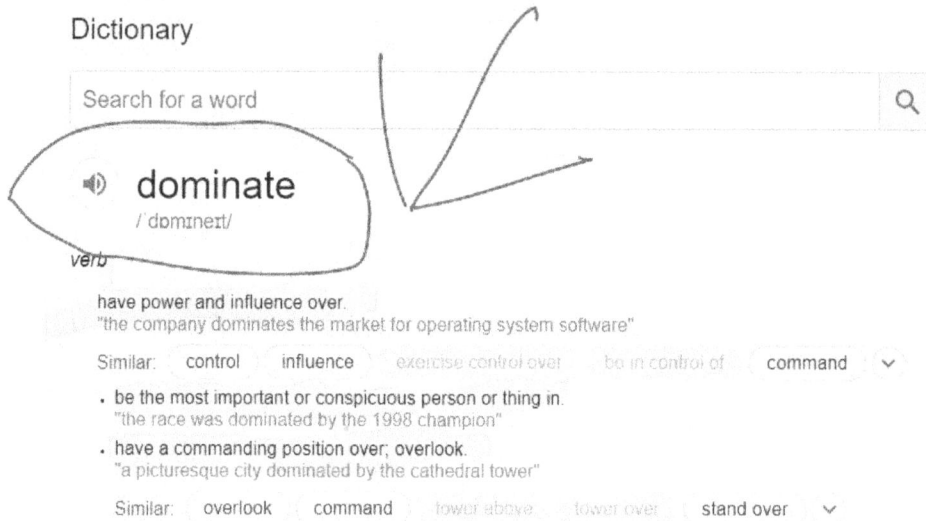

Dictionary

Search for a word

dominate
/ˈdɒmɪneɪt/

verb

have power and influence over.
"the company dominates the market for operating system software"

Similar: control influence exercise control over be in control of command

- be the most important or conspicuous person or thing in.
  "the race was dominated by the 1998 champion"
- have a commanding position over; overlook.
  "a picturesque city dominated by the cathedral tower"

Similar: overlook command tower above tower over stand over

If I show up on a Zoom or in person, I will be remembered for sure because I understand the mechanics of working a room. As you can see here, it is about being an influencer in your field of knowledge. If you have written a biography or a memoir, it is about being your authentic self. When people think of a certain topic, your name must come to mind, and you must be on the lips of your prospects and create a healthy buzz in your tribe. Even if you are a quiet, mild, meek, shy, timid person, you are going to have to learn to find your voice and say 'boo' to your target audience. STAND UP, STAND OUT and STEP FORWARD. Let them know you are here to stay.

Committing to Win

There is a reggae artist called Koffee who has a song called 'W' and the W stands for WIN. In the song, Koffee says, "Lowe di L, take di W". The same advice applies to you, focus on the mindset of the destination of where you want your book business to go. Success attracts opportunities and provides a platform to be recognised as an expert in your field. Do not worry about what you have not got; it is not worth it. Forget who did not buy your book; who is not supporting you; those who gave a bad review; or, those who call your name behind your back. People were not given the vision that God has placed inside of you. To create a legacy, you must run with your vision, without ceasing.

Committing to win means to be in a first-class premium position. It is less about being competitive and more about being your best self in all circumstances. Become an influencer within your chosen field. When you do something, do it well and with grace. To be honest, sometimes, in my personal experience, people become insecure because they feel threatened by your success, and that is sad. It is not about you; it speaks more about them. I believe that there is enough for everybody to eat and earn money. However, the trauma that some individuals have been through, especially recently, can cause them to want to stray off the path.

I can sit and tell you some stories about fake friends, haters, enemies, users, and frenemies; however, my time would not be well placed here, and our time here together is so valuable. I need to be focused on sharing what I know and giving you bite-size knowledge, insights, tips and wisdom to get you on the path of understanding your book marketing machine. It is crucial that I help as many authors as I can with my knowledge and expertise. This is what I want to give to the next generation of authors. a This is my talent! This is my gift! This is my skillset! I want to blaze and leave a trail behind me that significant and that says you can be a successful woman of colour, with sun kissed mocha skin. We deserve the same as our male counterparts and it is time that the corporate book industry starts levelling the playing field. I will never stop striving for excellence or attaining success or accolades. It is true, I like to push myself and see what I can create under pressure because after I die, this will be my legacy. Therefore, I encourage so many of you not only to get your books written but to earn an income and make a living from the sales of your book. The secret is to be fearless about your commitment to win and go after your dreams with fierce determination and vigour.

"Why are you struggling to fit in when you were born to stand out"?

Andy Harrington

How to Become an Amazon Number 1 Bestseller

Congratulations on making it to the end of the book! You have come a long way; I am so proud of your staying power. Well done! If you are like me, you probably would have skipped to the end to find out what the secret sauce was. That is a good thing; it means that you are curious enough to push forward, but remember, there is a process to everything. There are no such thing as overnight results, and you have got to put in the work.

Here is the thing, there is no profound secret. Sorry to disappoint you, that was not my intention, but real recognises real. So here it is: I was able to reach the number 1 bestseller on Amazon in the category of children's literature studies, simply because I did the math and correctly chose an obscure genre.

On one selected date, I sold enough books to hit the number one spot on Amazon because it is about compounding my sales in a short time. For you to reach the top 100, the top 40 or the top 10 and ultimately the coveted number 1 bestseller spot, you must have enough of your friends and family purchase your book on the same day. Once enough people have bought your book in your chosen category, it will be more likely to chart.

Amazon has hundreds of book categories online. They are split between non-fiction and fiction. You should become familiar with subjects. To get into the Amazon Top 10 at least, you must choose obscure categories, not necessarily ones that are unrelated to your book subject as it will spoil your algorithms of readers finding you, but definitely choose ones that are not popular. For example, the superhero category is extremely competitive, and we were able to reach number 2. Remember, Amazon chose this third category for us automatically. If I chose action heroes or selected adventures, that would have been a less competitive category, and it is likely to hit the number 1 spot.

Amazon has three different book categories it puts your book in. Two of them you select yourself in the online process of the upload of the book on KDP, and the last one they generate themselves based on keywords and your book description. Corporates Publishers buy in bulk and hire airport space to meet their sales targets; self-published authors do not have that privilege.

Now my secret sauce is out; you have worked hard to unlock the secrets. Now, make sure you go out and plan your day. Where are you going to get your fans, friends and family to support you to help you to hit the number 1 spot on Amazon or another bestseller list. Below is a list of the category headings on Amazon KDP, which breaks down into sub-headings for your perusal. The hard work now begins. Good luck, let me know how it goes.

Choose up to two categories: [x]

- [+] Fiction
- [+] Nonfiction
- [+] Juvenile Fiction
- [+] Juvenile Nonfiction
- [+] Comics & Graphic Novels
- [+] Education & Reference
- [+] Literary Collections
- [ ] Non-Classifiable

Selected Categories

Nonfiction > Business & Economics > Entrepreneurship Remove
Nonfiction > Self-Help > Motivational & Inspirational Remove

Cancel | Save

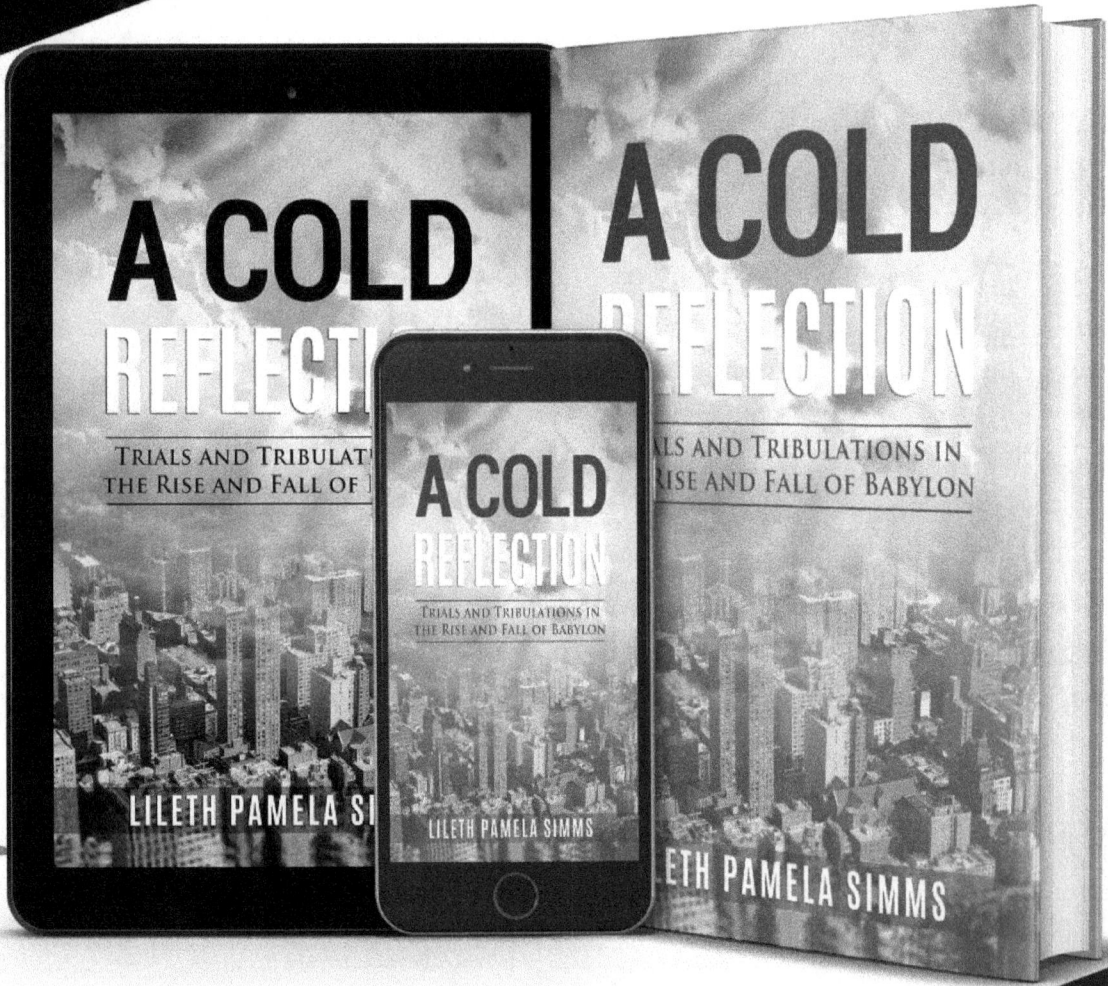

Epilogue

While I am still living and breathing on this planet, I feel compelled to share with you what I know. I want to teach others how to become publishers and earn their own income in their own rights. I believe in the importance of community group economics, and I want to see my people rise and earn money like their counterparts.

You see, the world is full of injustice at the moment; it is full of hate for the great leaders of our time; it is full of fear, and each one needs to teach one for all of us to advance. How can I rest when my brother or sister needs help in their journey? If anything, what I hope you get from reading this book is a sense of expansion and the conviction that this is the beginning of your marketing journey and that you will go on to have an inquiring mind and learn to be investigative and go onto YouTube and find out what it is that you do not know. As I said, if you are busy, outsource and pay somebody else to do it.

By now, you should understand that it takes courage, grit, and determination to get your book into the hands of people who will read it. I am sure that you want to stand out of the crowd; you have that singular voice that is unique for the world to hear. No one's story is like your story, so you must walk forth boldly into your destiny and into the vision of what you have been called to do. Approximately 60% of the people that read this workbook will be happily wishing and daydreaming of being bestseller status and making strides. However, that is all it will be, just a dream.

Always remember, you control your destiny in life and therein lies the power of the tongue, so make sure when you are moving forward in the marketing of your book and the building of your book business. Move forward boldly, earnestly, and full of creativity. Add excitement on the journey ahead. Good luck with completing your marketing strategy and do let me know how you are getting on with your book sales and share any questions you have here: www.facebook.com/groups/bookconfidencecoach.

Warmest regards,

Winsome Duncan

References

The following reference list is to help you on the next phase of your marketing journey. The list below are services that I have use myself and that you might find useful.

Hardback books: www.ingramspark.com	**Free and paid template website:** www.wix.com or www.weebly.com
Stormzy page: https://amzn.to/3r3PR65	**Free and paid template website**: www.weebly.com & www.wix.com
Marketing with Chandler Bolt: https://www.linkedin.com/in/chandlerbolt/	**Audio book recording**: please quote 'QUIRKY' to Lily when you contact her: www.lilymensah.com
Copy Writing: www.aniksingal.com	**Amazon Affiliates:** www.affiliate-program.amazon.co.uk
Design templates: https://www.canva.com/	**Kindlepreneur for Amazon book advertising:** www.youtube.com/c/Kindlepreneur/featured
Google ads: https://ads.google.com/	**Join Clubhouse App:** Currently on iPhone download only
Light Ring: https://amzn.to/3tViWT9	**Spell and grammar check:** https://app.grammarly.com/
Merchandise: www.vistaprint.co.uk	**Amazon Author Central:** https://author.amazon.co.uk/?locale=en_GB
Short edits and spellcheck: www.reverso.net	**Google**: Keyword Planner
Lulu: www.lulu.com	**Ty Cohen:** https://www.tycohen.com/

About the Author

Winsome Duncan – Award Winning Book Confidence Coach

Meet Number 1 Bestselling Author & Publisher

Winsome Duncan is one woman with a HUGE vision of getting her wider community writing books. She has more than 15 years' experience in the book publishing industry. As an author of 16 books, which includes her recent Amazon number 1 smash hit 'The Popcorn House', Winsome works tirelessly with budding Authors and Entrepreneurs to help them realise their book-writing dreams. She is the CEO of publishing house Peaches Publications and not for profit social enterprise the Look Like Me Book Challenge. Which has a particular focus on stories and voices from the Black community which include children age 7 – 18 years old.

Her latest project is a ground-breaking campaign called 'Look Like Me Book Challenge' which supports 30 Black, Asian & Minority Ethnic (BAME) children's authors to write one collective community book. Since the Guardian newspaper published that a mere 5% of BAME main characters are in children's books within the UK. This is compared to 33.5% of BAME school children in education. Inanimate objects are more likely to feature in children's books than Black or Brown faces. Winsome is passionate about changing this narrative and began fund-raising on her birthday weekend in October 2019 for £50,000 to help raise awareness and educate others about the importance of having equal visual representation for multicultural children from diverse heritage.

Winsome provides creative writing online courses and workshops for budding writers. As well as her prestigious JUST WRITE IT MASTERCLASSES at the Millennium Gloucester Hotel in Kensington and Chelsea, London.

Winsome Duncan Amazon Central Book Profile:
https://www.amazon.co.uk/Winsome-Duncan/e/B0034Q93UU/ref=dp_byline_cont_book_1

Motto: #wepublishbooks

For online course access with weekly lives visit:
www.bookconfidencecoach.com

**For more information about publishing your book
visit:** www.peachespublications.co.uk

For children storytelling workshops click here: www.looklikeme.co.uk.

Social Media Links:
Instagram: https://www.instagram.com/peachespublications/
Facebook: https://www.facebook.com/peachespublications/
Twitter: https://twitter.com/lyricalhealeruk
LinkedIn: https://www.linkedin.com/in/winsome-duncan-84622137/

THE JUST
WRITE IT
MODEL
SETTING YOUR INTENTION
INDUSTRY STANDARD CONTENTS PAGE
BEST-SELLING BOOK TITLES
JUST WRITE IT
amazon.com
BEST
SELLING
BOOK
Peaches
Publications
www.bookconfidencecoach.com

TELL YOUR STORY
WRITE YOUR BOOK
ONLINE COURSE
AUTHORS
EDITION
Peaches
Publications
amazon.com
BEST
SELLING
BOOK
www.bookconfidencecoach.com

About Lily Naadu Mensah

Sassy, spirited and motivational is the multi-award-winning brand called Lily Naadu Mensah! She is an internationally savvy personal brand connoisseur with a flair for creating a professional and endearing online presence, in person and on paper. Her consulting and speaking practice spans over twenty years across USA, Africa, and Europe. In her toolbox, Lily presents a collection of options for a 360° view of Brand-You. These are designed to increase visibility for personal and professional growth.

Lily is the Author of the Personal Branding book, *Work Your QUIRKs.*

For more information on branding for yourself or business, please contact Lily and quote '**QUIRKY**' via any of the following channels:

Email: lily@lilymensah.com

Website: www.lilymensah.com

Facebook: @ladymensahbrand

Instagram: @ladymensahbrand

LinkedIn: https://www.linkedin.com/in/ladymensah/

"Let your legacy be written in the walls of time."

The Popcorn House

Please continue to donate and support thirty children to create their audio book and animation from their number 1 bestselling story *'The Popcorn House'*.

https://www.gofundme.com/f/look-like-meBook-challenge

Appendix

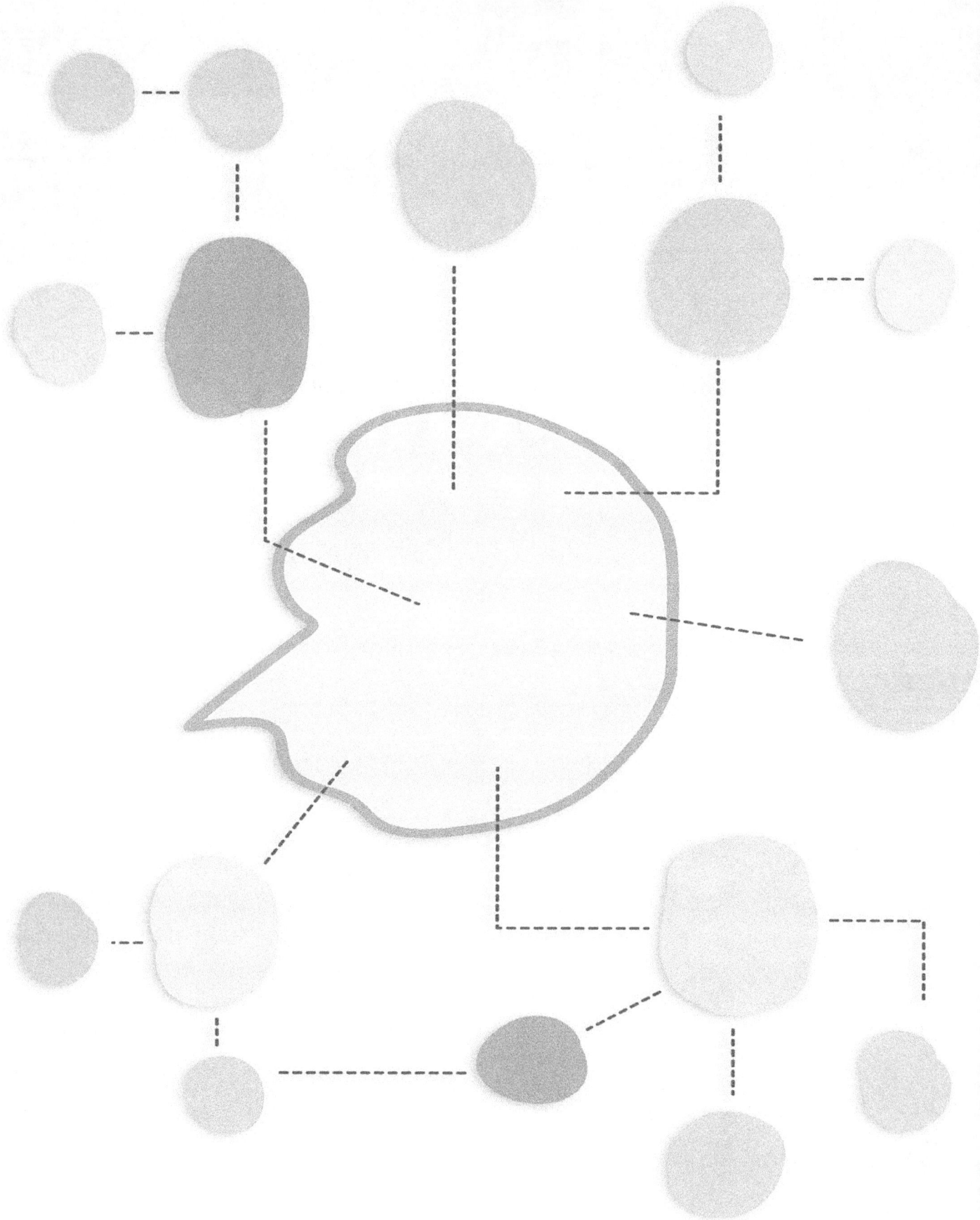

Just Market It

Mind Mapping

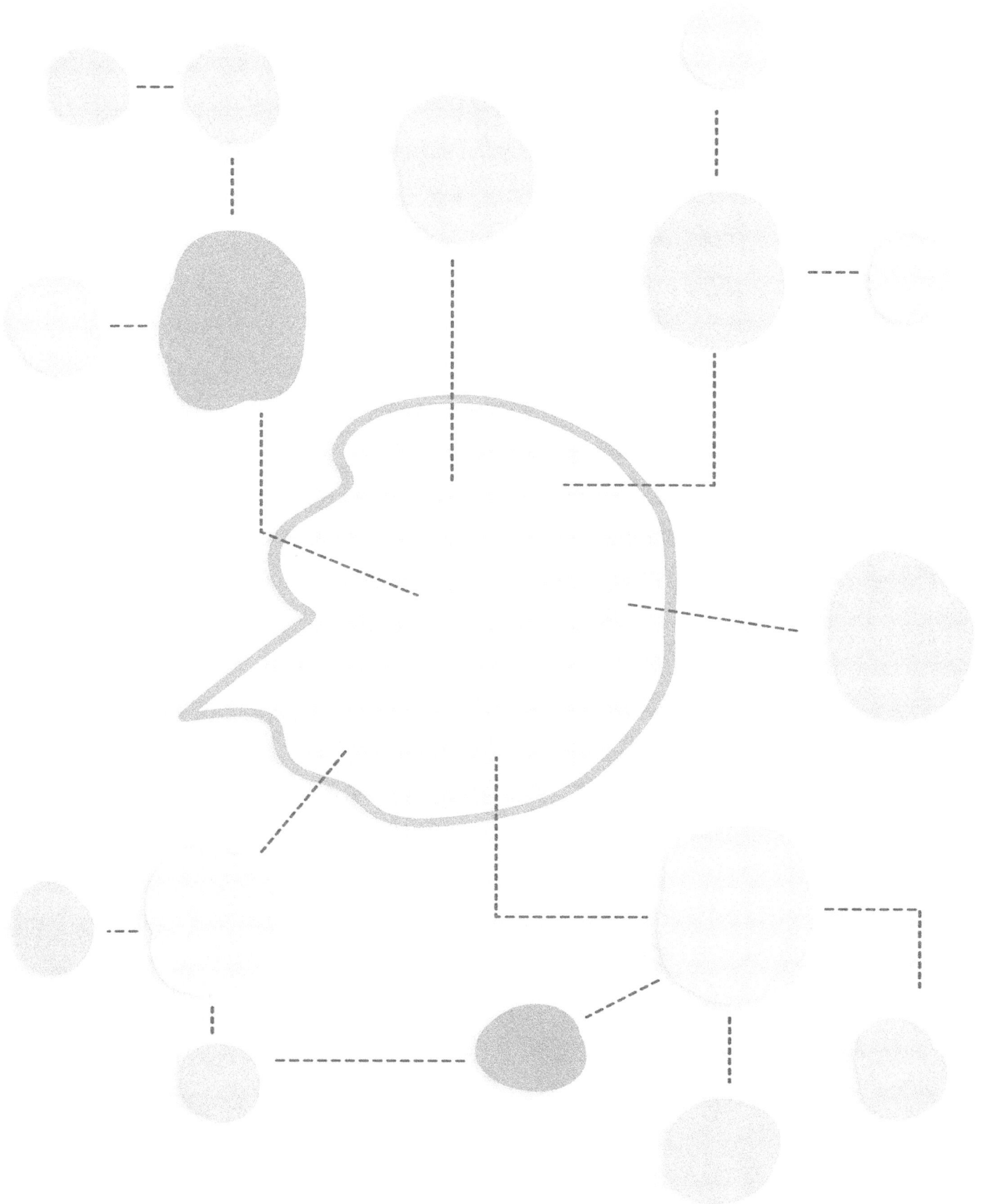

Just Market It

Mind Mapping

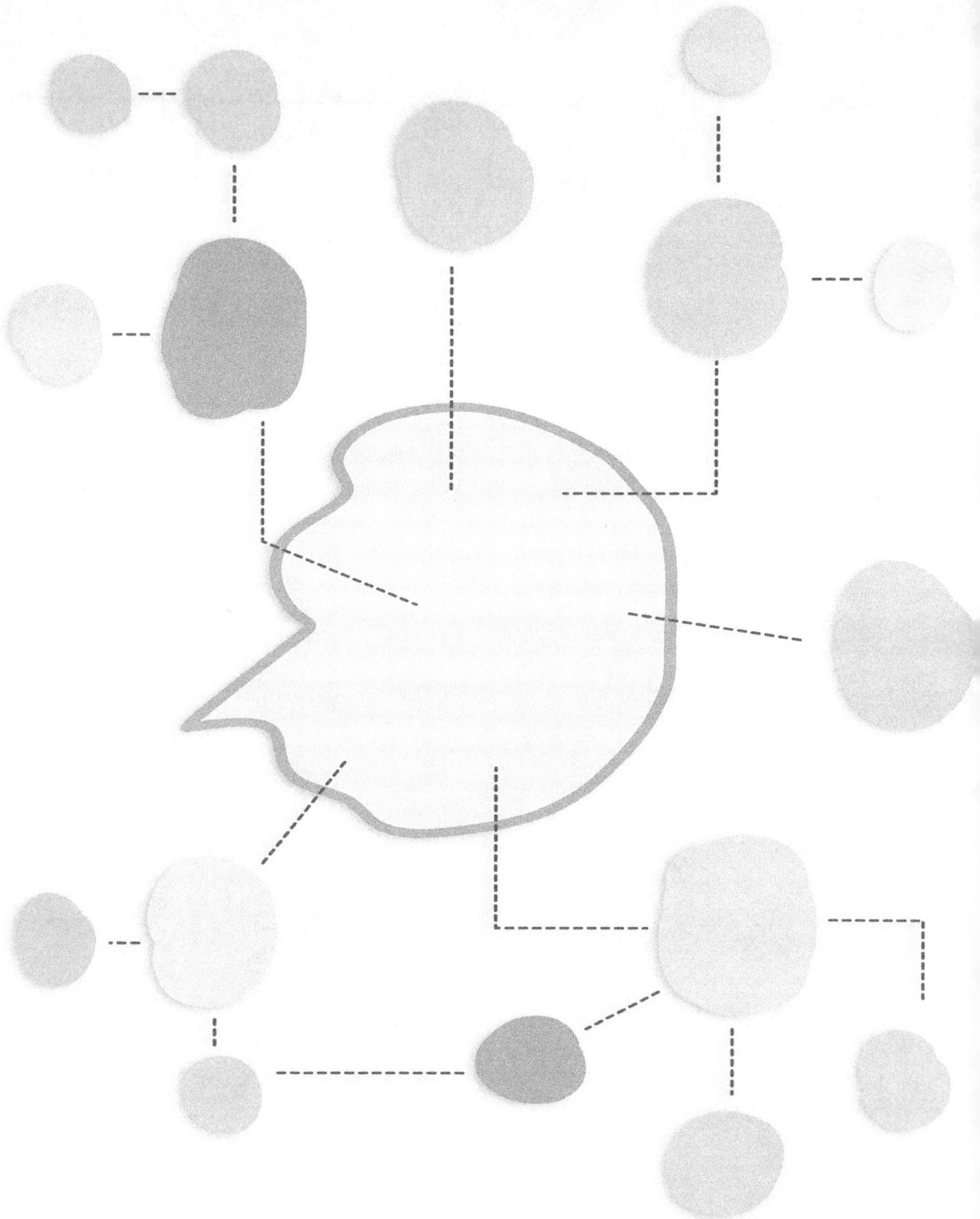

Just Market It

Mind Mapping

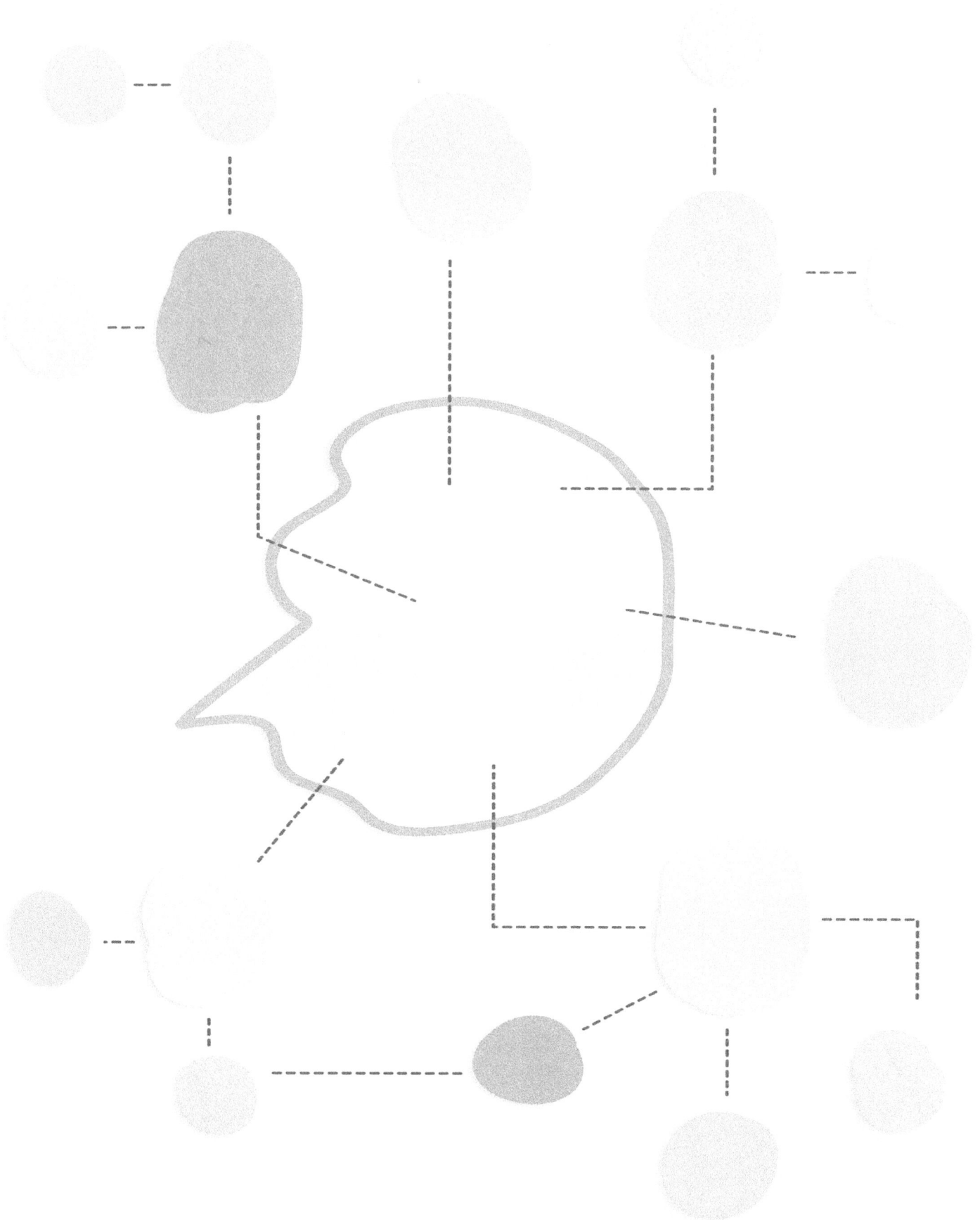

Just Market It

Mind Mapping

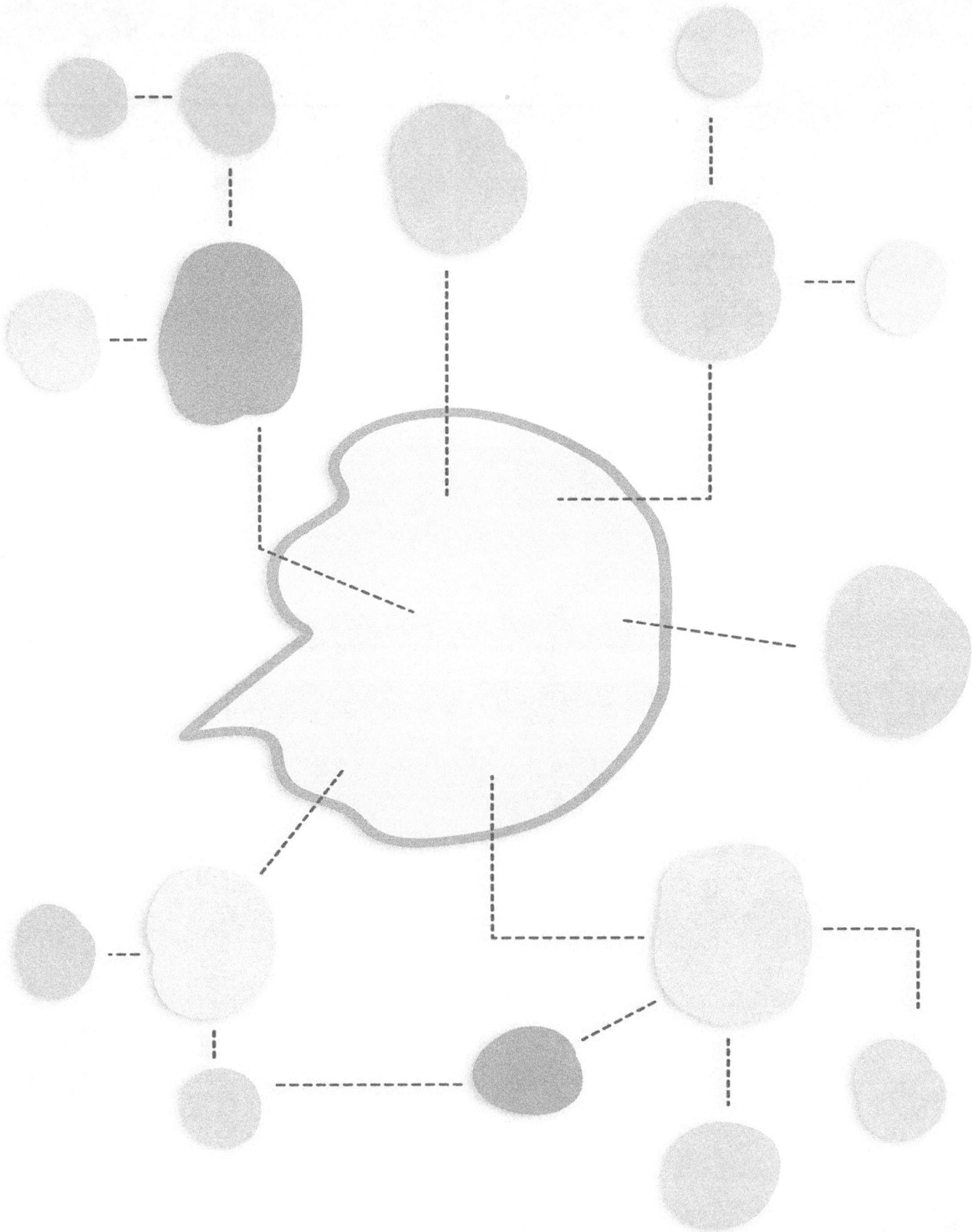

Just Market It

Mind Mapping

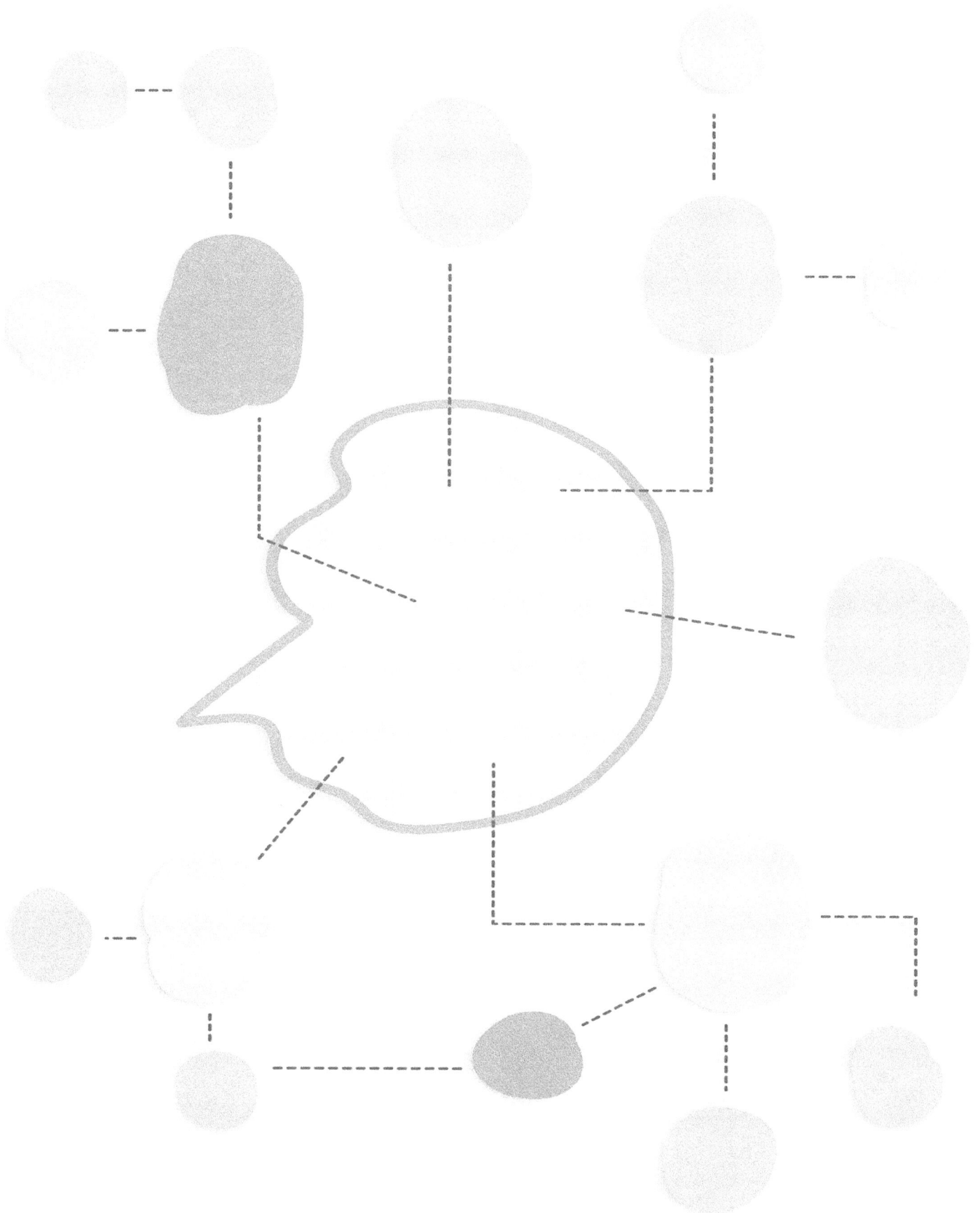

Just Market It

Mind Mapping

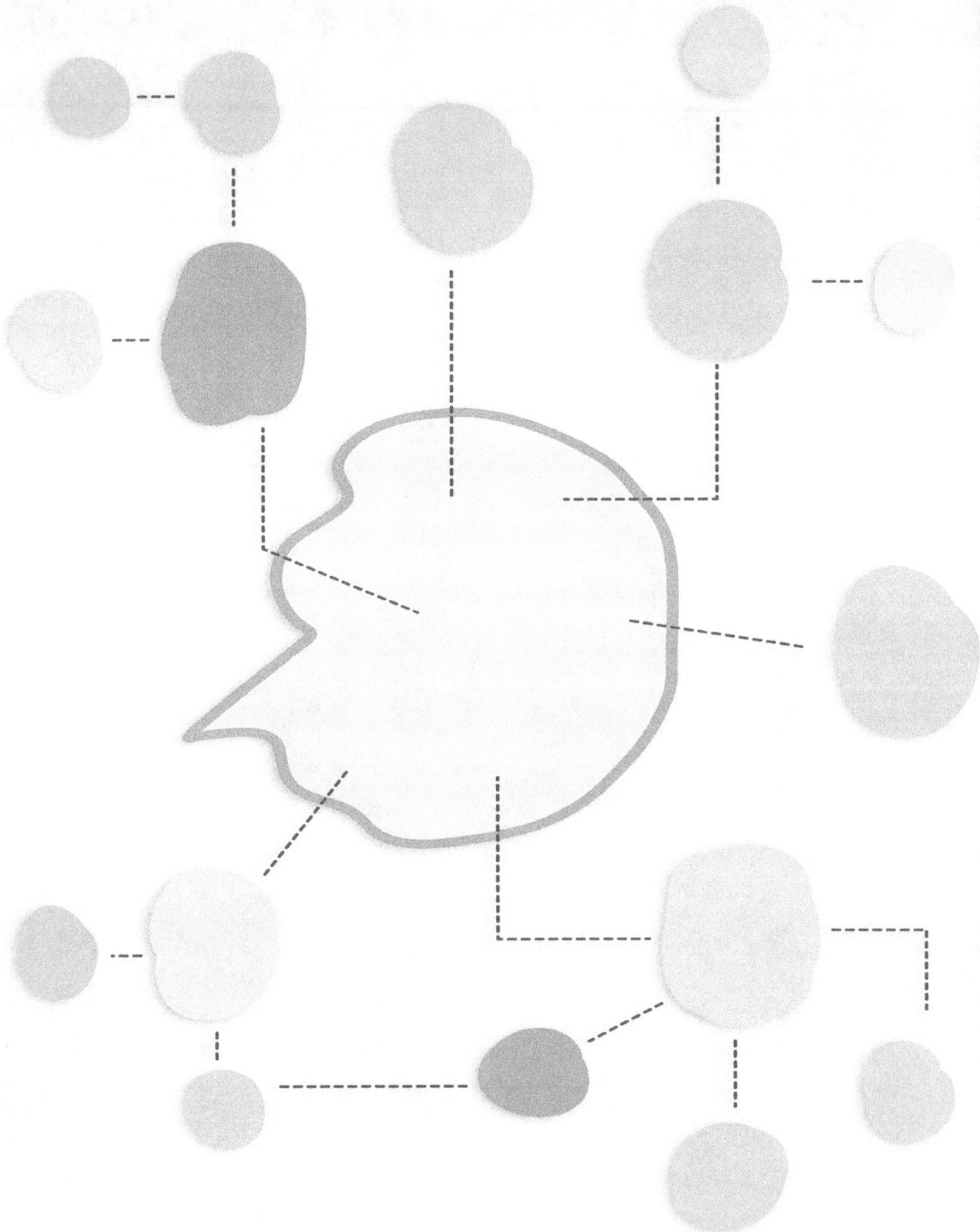

Just Market It

Mind Mapping

Study Notes

Study Notes

_____

_____

_____

_____

_____

_____

_____

_____

_____

_____

_____

_____

_____

_____

_____

_____

Study Notes

Study Notes

Study Notes

_____

_____

_____

_____

_____

_____

_____

_____

_____

_____

_____

_____

_____

_____

Study Notes

Study Notes

Study Notes

Study Notes

Study Notes

Just Market It

Study Notes

Study Notes

Study Notes

Study Notes

Study Notes

Study Notes

Study Notes

Study Notes

www.ingramcontent.com/pod-product-compliance
Lightning Source LLC
Chambersburg PA
CBHW051410200326

41520CB00023B/7179